SAVED

MW00696033

BUT

DAMAGED

KEYS TO EMOTIONAL HEALING

REVISED EDITION

DR. JERRY A. GRILLO, JR.

FZM Publishing
Copyright 2006
P.O. Box 3707 Hickory, N.C. 28603

Second Print 2007
Third Print 2011
Fourth Print 2014

All Scriptures, unless indicated, are taken from the King
James Version.

Scripture quotations marked NJKV are taken from the New
King James Version.

Scripture quotations marked NIV are taken from the New
International Version.

ISBN 978-0692274101

Printed in the United States of America

Table of Content

SPECIAL THANKS

I want to thank Dr. Mike Murdock for all the mentor moments he spent with me through the years. A lot of what I teach is a result of his training and guidance. We are all a compilation of those who have poured into our lives. No one can escape the power of a good mentor. I do not apologize for it, but embrace the power of teaching and learning.

I want to thank my parents for being there and supporting me throughout my life. Mom and Dad, I honor and value every moment we spend together. You are a source of joy and strength.

I want to also thank my precious and most loyal companion and friend, my wife Maryann. You're strong girl! I thank God for that strength. You have been the wind beneath my wings. I love you dearly! And to my two wonderful, awesome children, Jerry and Jordan, I love hanging out with you. Daddy loves you with all his heart.

Last but not least… Jesus Christ, the Son of God. You are the source of all I do. Where would I be if You hadn't stayed with me? Through thick and thin You are truly the power of greatness. I love you most of all!

PREFACE

Churches have become feel-good carnivals with cheerleading and positive pumped-up messages. We've watered down our principles to make the hurting and worldly feel more comfortable. I'm not advocating that all churches have fallen into this trap, but I think that there are more than we'd like to admit. There's little or no distinction between what is worldly and what is Godly.

Comfort probably wasn't what God had in mind when He designed the power of preaching. Preaching the Gospel was meant to bring hope through all things, but not comfort at all cost. Preaching was designed to bring us back into God's perspective, showing us that we are not lining up with His principles and laws. Sermons were designed to convict those who've ignored what they were called to do; to show them mercy and a way back. It was to be a message leading people to the cross; a message for the lost and their need for Jesus.

Preaching wasn't to be colored, colored-faded or pastels. The truth was to be preached in black and white with no gray areas, no seeker safeness to its reality. The truth was *suppose* to make the ungodly uncomfortable!

But now we have made comfort our focus and real salvation an afterthought.

COMFORT: Comfort means feeling no difference when leaving one atmosphere for another. For example, most of us have central heat and air. Central heating and air conditioners were invented to make the house comfortable. It was designed to give us unified comfort in all rooms. You can leave the living room and enter the bedroom without adjusting your clothing to remain cool or warm. This is exactly what we've done with our churches; we've made them accustomed to the world.

We've attempted to make the worldly comfortable with the church, hoping that we could thereby win them to Christ. But the comfortable church is not distinguishable from the world; there's no climate change from one place to the other. The world can walk into church without having to make any adjustments. So people come and leave the same as always.

We're making confessions of faith and we believe for salvation, but we're neglecting the emotional state of those who are being saved – *saved but damaged*. We need to understand that people can be saved from hell, but not be set free from what has hurt and wounded them in their past.

Although God can touch and save us from our sins, He can do little with our wounds if we keep them from Him. We are saved, but we still need to be made whole. Healed but not whole is a dangerous place. Saved but still damaged can eventually destroy our walk with God. We need to recognize and admit that we are damaged. It's this recognition that keeps our wounds from bleeding into our present season.

So whether you're reading this book because you have wounds or because you know someone who does, take your time. I have labored to give you the necessary steps to start your healing. I have prayed over each word and I believe with the Lord, the Bible, and this book you are on your way to emotional healing.

In your walk towards healing, don't allow those who hurt you to remain in your life. Stop helping those who pull you down. If you are emotionally wounded face the mess of your life so God can turn your life into a message.

It takes courage to put order into chaos, and I am confident that you will possess that courage once you have finished reading this book. These pages have been prayed over. I sense that the hand of God is on each and everyone. Take your time. Healing is coming!

I am grateful that you are reading this book. I truly believe that it will help you reach your God-given destiny.

Dr. Jerry A. Grillo, Jr.

CHAPTER ONE

I'M SAVED
BUT
DAMAGED

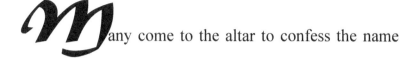any come to the altar to confess the name

of Jesus, lugging with them wounds, scars, shame, guilt and pain from divorce, abuse, molestation, rape, neglect, anger, insecurities, inferiorities, religious hurts, fear, low self–esteem, addictions, homosexuality, murder, and more. And they leave the altar undeniably "saved" from hell and damnation. But are they saved from life and its horrors as they've known it? Do they leave changed and whole to embrace life more abundant than ever before?

Probably not, because the one thing they forgot at the altar was the invitation to be made whole; to trade the sorrow, shame, pain, wounds, and hurts of their bodies, minds, and spirits for healing and wholeness through Jesus Christ. Yes they've left "saved," but they've also left carrying the heavy burden filled with all past pains and disappointments back with them. They try to climb to new heights in their new-found salvation only to find that the weight of their past baggage is hindering them.

It's not that our churches aren't the ideal places for them to succeed, to become saved, healed, and fixed. It's just that no one seems to be willing to address those heavy burdens many are dragging back and forth. We just keep preaching and singing and hoping that the emotionally wounded will leave their smelly baggage somewhere, discover their healing and be set free.

My heart aches as I see so many leave the altar *Saved But Still Damaged,* which is the very reason I have labored to write this book. I've labored to fill these pages with God's truths and encouragement in great hopes of helping many achieve the wholeness promised them.

If we do not disciple and guide those who've become saved, they will try to live their saved life the same way they've lived their damaged life, using the same flawed mindsets... the same reasoning... the same attitudes... the same temperament... etc.

Our churches are full of hurting, insecure, messed-up people who cannot understand why they just can't break free from their problems. They fail to realize that they have yet to face and destroy their damaged perception of what has messed them up, and what keeps tripping them up.

Perhaps this book is for you. Perhaps you've had an angry, abusive father or mother... perhaps you're the victim of a sexual offense... perhaps someone you've trusted has betrayed you... whatever or whoever has caused you pain, you are not to blame. Not now, not then! Perhaps you're stuck in the prison of your mind, surrounded by walls of painful memories and bars of doubt which these wrongs have created.

You are either going to live the rest of your life in the prison of your pain or in the palace of your freedom. The only one who can choose which of the two it will be **is you!** Why do you remain at the bottom of your debilitating condition when you should be sitting at the table with the King? Don't let your condition rob you of your entitlement to be with the King and receive His blessings.

Animals that have been in captivity for years are said to remain in their cages after they are given a chance to escape. The pitiful animals just sit there… free, but still caged to a memory! Caged animals cannot comprehend that the doors which held them captive for so long have been opened, so they stay imprisoned behind opened doors. Is that you? Has God opened your prison doors, but you remain caged to the painful memories of your damaged caged life? Listen! COME OUT OF THE CAGE! You have been set free! You're saved and you shall not stay damaged!

Is it possible that your body was freed but your mind is still stuck in the prison of your pain? In these times, counseling and mental problems seem to be more the norm than the deviant. Psychology has increasingly come into focus since the late fifties. The thought behind it was that so many were depressed as a result of guilt because society's standards and values were set too high, too

> **ONLY THE HOLY SPIRIT CAN REPRINT ON YOUR MIND THE NECESSARY CHANGES THAT WILL HEAL YOUR EMOTIONAL WOUNDS.**

unattainable. It was thought that society was unable to fulfill or meet its high moral standard. The solution seemed obvious. Lower the moral standard put upon mankind thereby eliminating guilt and depression.

The answer proved that people became even more depressed and more mentally wounded than ever before. The theory remained intact, but the solution was flawed. It never was God's plan for us to attain such high moral standards alone and without help. Real help was not to be attained by simply lowering the standards. God wants us to become "born again," born in the Spirit. God intended us to be full of something much greater than mere human ability and reasoning. God provided us with the answer, but apart from this answer neither you nor I can fulfill the requirement of reaching such height of perfection. The very answer to our dilemma was, is and forever will be Jesus!

We are not able to walk free of our hurts and pains without Jesus. Modern-day church has us learning without ever coming to the point of truth. That truth is Jesus. He is what all truth should point to. If we are learning for any other reason but Jesus, we are learning for all the wrong reasons.

Consider that all of our knowledge, all of our rapidly expanding technology, all of our great feats and accomplishments seem to have only pushed us further away from God. We should have come closer unto Him. How can this be? We're drifting because we are gaining knowledge with the "Tower of Babel curse" in our hearts. We are gaining and doing with one motive and that motive being only for our name's sake.

"And they said, Go to, let us build us a city and a tower, whose top may reach unto heaven; and let us make us a name, lest we be scattered abroad upon the face of the whole earth." Genesis 11:4 KJV

Whenever we attempt to build our knowledge to attain heaven, while at the same time trying to build a name for ourselves, we build not for the Kingdom of God but for the kingdom of "self." We can't do both. Only in God can both become possible. For instance, God tells Abraham to leave his comfort and to follow Him (Gen.12:1). Then God tells Abraham, "If you do this I will make your name great" (Gen. 12:2). God desires that we become healed and delivered so that we can do and become great for His Kingdom. However, we must first abandon ourselves for His gain and show Him that we can be trusted with His assignments and blessings. While we are in the process of releasing our stuff, God is releasing His blessings back to us.

There cannot be real healing if such is for our selfish benefit only; however, healing is inevitable for that which God has preordained us for.

Many storm the altar confessing the Name of Jesus in search of a quick fix. Many want instant relief of their present pains and will only come to church as long as they can do so without further discomfort. They'd rather not face their painful pasts; they'd rather not open doors to things that have caused them much grief and pain. God can have them as long as He doesn't come too uncomfortably close; as long as He doesn't try to expose or touch their sore spots in an attempt to heal or change them. This is the mentality of the 21st Century believer. "I will do and come as long as I don't have to change." *THEY ARE SAVED BUT STILL WOUNDED*.

Allow me to ask one very important question. How can God really use you if you are still messed up? Should

God put you in the path of those who are hurting, if you yourself are not healed from what has wounded you? Hurting people eventually hurt people.

Examine yourself, your environment and your life. Is it really what you've intended it to be? Are you all that you can be? If others don't esteem to be like you, if no one seems to take your advice, then maybe it's because you're not as together, as fixed, or as healed as you'd like to appear.

I know people who have been church goers for most of their lives, yet they are mean-spirited. They confess to be saved yet they are full of unforgiveness, bitterness, and hatred. There's little or no joy in their faces, and all they want to do is complain. How can they really believe to be ok? Because they've lived the lie for so long they have turned it into the truth. But it's only their truth, not the true truth. In light of the real truth (namely Jesus) they are a lie!

Saved but damaged!

Where are the saved and healed Christians hiding? There is a process to emotional healing. You will first have to understand that *you are not better by your standards. You are only better when someone else says you're better.* Follow the pattern which I have outlined in the next chapters and you will be on your way to emotional healing.

CHAPTER TWO

WOUNED PEOPLE LEAK ISSUES!

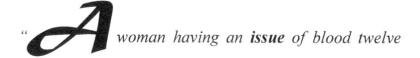 *woman having an **issue** of blood twelve years, which had spent all her living upon physicians, neither could be healed of any..." Luke 8:43 KJV*

This woman had a problem that lasted twelve years. She had an issue of blood which means that she was hemorrhaging or bleeding. She had neither power nor resources to cure her problem. Her issue had cost her dearly. This is what unresolved issues will do. They will begin to drain you of all your resources, physically, mentally and spiritually.

The phrase *"neither could be healed of any..."* causes me to drift into her world. I can't imagine having this kind of pain for twelve long years, searching for an answer, a cure, relief. She had no answer and yet she was full of questions. What a hard and sad place it must be to be full of questions and find no one with an answer as to what's been ailing and killing you for years.

I wonder if the woman with the issue of blood sat up that very morning shuddering with the stark reality that she was growing worse even after having spent her all on every physician she could find. She was forbidden by her culture to enter into contact with other people. She was commanded by law to announce her entry and to let others know of her problem. This must have been embarrassing, isolating and banishing; people snubbing her at every turn.

Isn't that exactly what happens to those who still harbor hurts and wounds, issues of the past? No matter how hard they try to mask them, somehow the sores erupt ruining what could've been a good time or a good relationship. The woman turned to others for help to solve her problem, her crisis, her bleeding and her pain, but found that people couldn't stop the leakage. When you are hurting, other people usually can't help you either.

People aren't the answer. God is. The woman heard that Jesus was coming to her village that day. Perhaps she was hopeful that He would walk near her home. Whatever the scenario might have been, she did what she needed to do. She pushed herself toward Him. She mustered up enough strength to get dressed, to fight the crowd and to make one last attempt to find her peace...her healing... her resolve. Are you willing to gather your strength to do just that?

Where was this peace she hungered for? It was locked

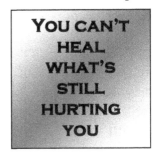

within the Son of God. When she finally saw Jesus, she got down on her hands and knees and pressed... pushed... and heaved her tired yet determined self to Him. I believe that her faith unlocked what was in Jesus' spirit; that her pursuit got His attention. The proof of desire is pursuit.

That day the woman found the answer to her wound and that answer was **JESUS!** If you suffer from a wound or issue do what this lady did. Press your way through your shame, pain and hang-ups and get to Jesus. Give Him your issues and leave them there with Him. God will take care of your past.

Hurting people hurt people! We've learned how to mask externally what's been destroying us internally. In the case of the woman with the issue of blood, this internal hemorrhaging was leaking her life's substance. Remember, she had spent all that she had on people yet grew worse. **That's because people were not the healing agent in her life.**

People can't be the healing agent in your life because more than likely they have issues themselves. You can't effectively help others until you are healed yourself. You can't claim your future if you haven't released your past. You can't pick up a diamond as long as you're clutching your axe. You can't hold new wine if your wineskin is brittle and leaks.

Wounds leak! Wounds that never heal always find a way to be opened. Leakage will keep people from living a full and fulfilling life. A wife who hasn't forgiven her father will never fully love her husband. A husband who has never forgiven his mother will harbor resentment toward his wife. A son who was hurt by his father can't seem to find wholeness in his children. Wounded people leak. They leak their life's substance. They leak their hurt on anyone who comes close enough to listen.

Leaking people usually ruin relationships because others can only bear to be leaked on for a season. No matter how good such a relationship begins, it will end in a mess. Some signs of an unhealed wound can be anger, bitterness, or jealousy.

DO OTHERS FEEL YOUR THORNS OR YOUR LOVE WHEN THEY GET CLOSE TO YOU?

"So He came to a city of Samaria which is called Sychar..." John 4:5 NKJV

The Bible introduces us to a woman who lived in the village of *Sycha* who would come to Jacob's well daily. One day Jesus sat waiting for her at that same well. We know that He was waiting for her because in earlier verses we find Him saying that He needed to go through Samaria. Jesus was on a divine assignment, an assignment not geared toward crowds of thousands but toward the heartbeat of one individual in dire need for change. She was a woman with all kinds of relational baggage. She had been married five times and admitted living with a sixth man who was not her husband.

It gives me chills to discover the Greek translation of Samaria and Sychar. "**Samaria**" means "**a hedge with thorns**," and "**Sycha**" means "**intoxicated as of a strong drink – to be influenced.**"

The woman at the well was being influenced by what was, not by what could've been. Her past hurts, past pains and past mistakes had intoxicated her to her past. Her hedge of hurt and pain had grown and she learned how to trim those hedges to make them look pretty. We can all become experts at trimming our hedges to make things within them seem properly spruced and in order. The truth of the matter is that this woman was not okay.

She had been with six men, five of whom she had married, one of whom she was shacking up with. Her pretty trimmed hedges were full of thorns! Her thorns were only exposed when people tried to get close to her, and her pain became their pain as soon as they pressed up against her.

IS HALF ENOUGH TO CHANGE?

The woman at the well was a Samaritan, meaning that she was half Jew and half Philistine. This meant that half of her was okay, but the other half was costing her. I believe that she was crying out to God saying, *"I know I'm half a mess, but the other half of me is Hebrew. Oh God, is half of me enough to get your attention? I'm no longer dreaming but stuck in this nightmare! God, I know I'm not allowed in Your building. Would You please come and visit me even for just one day? God, I need you! I need someone who can stop my cycle of mess and pain. Oh God, Help!"* What do you think God's answer was? You will find it in the following verse:

"But He needed to go through Samaria..." John 4:4-5 NKJV

Jesus needed to go through Samaria. Why? Because *she* was there! She became His audience, His assignment that day. Jesus came to Samaria to fix her wounds and change her life. Imagine... if that's what God did for a Samaritan, what could He be doing for you right now?

THE ART OF REJECTION: *REJECTION ALWAYS HURTS*

This woman in Samaria had been married five times. It is important to understand the culture in which she was living. Women didn't divorce their husbands. Women did not have that kind of control. So this certain woman was living the life of rejection; first, rejected because of her race, then rejected by five men who threw her out, and rejected by those in Samaria.

Women in that time didn't go to the well alone for fear of being attacked, yet here she was alone. **Rejection** is a powerful and damaging wound.

She was willing to settle for anyone because of rejection. She was not married at this point; just living with anyone who would accept her. Rejection will cause you to settle. I believe that one of the reasons that King David wouldn't kill King Saul, even when God placed Saul into his hands, was because Saul gave David something his biological father never gave him. David's father and brothers rejected him because he wasn't like the others. His difference caused his immediate family to reject him, but Saul and his sons accepted David. Saul filled a heart that was hurting. David found himself sitting at Saul's table laughing and feeling accepted for the first time.

Rejection will cause you to love those who hate you and hate those who love you. Rejection cuts deep, lives long, drives you to do crazy things and seek anyone who will accept you no matter how they treat you.

Maybe your wound has, for a time, thrown you into the ditch of despair and pain. Perhaps your wound has left you half dead. When an enemy leaves you wounded and dying, he often assumes your demise, not realizing that his infliction can become the steppingstone to your change and healing. You may be half dead, but you're also **still half alive**, which is enough for God! God can help you become what He has always preordained you to be. Don't give up! God is sitting on the well of your pain, your hurt, your past. He's there! Why? Because He needs to be there, not just for you, but for His Kingdom purpose, for the purpose of life...all life as He intended it to be... abundant, whole, full of joy, and everlasting. God knows that when He fixes you He also changes those around you, those connected to you and those who are stuck in nightmares searching for answers.

"And many of the Samaritans of that city believed in Him because of the word of the woman who testified, 'He told me all that I ever did." John 4:39-40 NKJV
Her mess became her message. Her changed life changed a city.

INFLUENCES THAT STOP CHANGE:

RELIGION:

This woman wasn't allowed to go to the local church because she was a Samaritan. Samaritans were half breeds. They were half Philistine and half Hebrew. So even if she desired to enter the house of God to lay down her burdens to the Lord she was not allowed to.

Religion hates better than it loves. Religion can stop the process of change. Religion is man's attempt to please God man's way.

RELATIONSHIPS:

What you hang out with, you will eventually become. Not everyone in your life belongs in your life. Those around you can be costing you dearly.

"Do not be misled: "Bad company corrupts good character." Come back to your senses as you ought, and stop sinning; for there are some who are ignorant of God-I say this to your shame." 1 Corinthians 15:33-34 NIV

Stop chasing those God is trying to exit out of your life.

RACIAL IGNORANCE:

Racial issues are deadly. Talk about racism! This Samaritan woman wasn't even allowed to enter the house of God. She couldn't even talk to a pure Jew. They were to stay away from her. Don't let the color of someone's skin stop you from moving into your destiny. When we cross the blood line, we should have dealt with the race line.

CONDITION:

Your condition could be costing you your position. We all have hurts. We all have skeletons in our closets. If God opened our past up to others we would all hide. She was wounded and so are we. We could be missing our chance for change because we are more focused on the wound than the way out. Don't let your condition rob you any longer.

THE INABILITY TO RECOGNIZE:

If we fail to recognize who God has sent to deliver us we will be stuck in our situation a long time. Her wounds were blocking her ability to see. She couldn't see that Jesus wasn't concerned about her race, religion, condition or her relationships. He was there to set her free from her past.

Dr. Murdock calls it The Law of Recognition. Anything unrecognized goes uncelebrated. Anything uncelebrated goes unrewarded. Anything unrewarded will exit your life.

What caused her to change? I believe there were four things she was willing to do that caused her change.

- **Her willingness to be corrected (vs. 17).**

  She allowed Jesus to expose her mistakes. She didn't become offended as so many do today. No, she listened and then she began to thirst for living water. Correction brings connection. The ones who correct you connect you to their future. When your mentor stops correcting you he disconnects from you because your future no longer matters to him.

- **Her willingness to ask the right question (vs. 19).**

  The woman at the well didn't ask, "Can you stop this pain?" She didn't ask Jesus for money or new things. Her question was a question of worship.

She asked, "Where can I worship? Where can I find a place to worship?" She was saying, "I need a place where I can lay my burdens on something bigger than myself." When she opened the subject of worship, revealing her desire to worship, Jesus never mentioned her sin again.

- **Her willingness to re-enter her past to bring change to her future (vs. 39).**

She was willing to return to her village to re-enter her past to secure her future and inevitably the future of many people from her past. Until you deal with your past, your future is not available. I'm not suggesting that you get rid of your past because without your past your future would have no meaning. You may even hate your present situation. Many do. Let me encourage you; until you hate your present, your future will not materialize.

- **Her willingness to release what she had, to obtain what Jesus had (vs. 28).**

"The woman then left her water pot…" Why did she leave without her pot? Because it was all that she had; it was the only seed she could sow. The woman released what she had so that God could replace her seed with His seed, which was Jesus. Jesus then released her harvest. The fastest way out of your crisis is a seed. ***"Keep thy heart with all diligence; for out of it are the issues of life."*** Proverbs 4:23 KJV

The word "issue" in Proverbs refers to "**boundaries**." Guard your heart, which is your mind. Therefore guard your mind! The boundaries of your life will come out of your mind. Past wounds will control your present and destroy the doorway to your future if you do not allow them to heal. You will not be able to walk into your God-given assignment until you've dealt with your pains… your wounds… your betrayals…etc.

A clue to your assignment is what you are healed from.

CHAPTER THREE

EMOTIONAL WOUNDS CAN PRODUCE INSECURITIES

THE WORLD SAYS YOU ARE WHO YOU ARE.

I SAY YOU ARE WHO GOD CREATED YOU TO BE.

 *" competent and self-confident person is*

incapable of jealousy in anything. Jealousy is invariably a symptom of neurotic insecurity." Robert A. Heinlein

Emotional wounds can be far more crippling than any physical injury. Victims of violence often suffer life-long consequences, physical as well as emotional. Therefore, to gauge the depth of the loss and the human tragedy, we must look further than the loss of life and limb.

"Death is viewed as the ultimate loss, but it's not necessarily the most painful thing. We measure the size of a catastrophe by the number of the people who lost their lives. Survivors are described as 'lucky.' But is everyone who survives lucky? Not always. In some cases death would have been more merciful than a life sentence of despair and darkness." *Vijai P. Sharma, Ph.D*

Wounds of past traumas often rob people of living a full and fulfilling life. Persons who have been wounded are unfulfilled because they are robbed of five basic emotional needs:

SAFETY: Having a sense of safety means trusting or believing that "my loved ones and I are safe." Victims constantly worry that something bad will happen either to them or their loved ones. This creates a constant state of tension. For example, a victim will assume the absolute worst whenever their spouse or child is late in returning home. Victims who refuse to let go of their past live in constant fear for their own safety and for the safety of those they love. Imagine the nightmare of always having to worry about those you love.

TRUST: Trust means believing that, "I can rely on myself and those around me" which creates security. Victims believe the following, "I can't trust myself because I can't protect myself." They tend to feel suspicious of others' motives and experience constant anxiety in the presence of strangers. Victims must learn how to open up and trust again. We'll deal more on "trust" further into the book.

CONTROL: Having control means believing that, "I can control what happens in my life and can influence others' behaviors towards me." Victims believe that they have no control over their lives and merely try to survive the injuries others have inflicted on them, which causes them to become overly controlling. They tend to restrict freedom, not allowing it to be a normal, necessary part of their lives, restricting especially the lives of those who have been placed into their care.

SELF-ESTEEM: Esteem means believing that, "I am loveable and that others can be loveable too." Having experienced intense hate by a perpetrator during acts of violence will often destroy that belief. Self criticism, self-dislike and even self-hate result from such interpersonal pain and wounds.

INTIMACY: Intimacy, or *'In-to-me-see,'* means that you

can open yourself up to another person and allow them to see what's inside. Some victims will shun emotional contact or closeness because they no longer trust themselves or others. They develop a life of being and feeling alone. Fear of being hurt again or of having to relive a past pain keeps them from opening themselves to others.

Such is the emotional cost of so many in our world. It saddens me to see the hollow eyes of the wounded in our churches as they look upward wondering why God can't stop their pain. They fail to realize that they must allow God to enter to stop the pain. Many physical ailments and life-long illnesses can occur from unresolved wounds.

INSECURITIES COULD BE COSTING YOU DEARLY.

Emotional wounds usually produce insecurities and identity crises. Persons who have insecurities live life with a sense of fear, anxiety and lack of confidence. They always seem to be apprehensive, not reliable and undependable. They are not well rooted or secure in life. To the contrary, they are quite insecure.

Insecurities, inferiorities, inadequacies, low self-esteem, bitterness, anger and relational baggage are some of the offspring of emotional wounds. They all interfere with our attainment of hope. Hope is necessary for us to grow fruitful and productive spiritual lives. Depression occurs when there is an absence of **hope**. Some say that people who have lost all hope become suicidal. They believe that their present life can never change for the better.

The absence of hope causes them to fall into depression and thoughts of suicide. The reality is their life can always change. The difference is how they see it. Is their event defining them or do they define the event? The difference between hope and hopelessness is how you see the events that are happening to you. They are either defining how you feel and what you believe or you are defining them. This event I am experiencing isn't my reality, it is my journey.

Hope means trusting that our wants and wishes will come true... desires accompanied by expectation. Hope is trust and reliance. When we live a life of insecurities, we rob ourselves of hope. Hope is what faith is built on. Without faith nothing from heaven can be released into our life. We must deal with our insecurities.

To be insecure means to be filled with anxieties, apprehensive, not firm or dependable, unreliable. Those who are suffering from insecurities have no self-esteem or confidence in their own abilities. When the insecure are given difficult tasks or have to endure complex trials, they will most likely give up and quit. They are not dependable. Their unhealed life costs them and those around them dearly.

An identity crisis is different. It is the condition of being uncertain of one's own feelings, especially in regard to character, goals, and origin. Identity crises often occur in adolescence as direct results of growing up under disruptive, fast-changing conditions.

Wounds of your past can cause you to build feelings of inadequacy, dubbing you as "not good enough." They can instill in you the belief that no one really cares. Past wounds can cause haunting questions like, "Why should anyone love me? Who am I? Why am I here?" These are questions that only you can answer; questions that should have been dealt with in adolescence. Your feelings of inadequacy are not based on truth, and although your feelings are very real and painful, they are not the result of reality. It is not my desire to belittle your feelings, but to shed light on the truth.

FACTS ABOUT INSECURITIES:

1. When you're healed of your insecurities, the need to compete with someone else will cease.

2. The need to see others fail is proof that you are still not completely healed of your insecurities.

3. As long as you're unsure of your own identity, you'll cheer others' failures because you need them to be less than you are.

4. You can develop your identity by fighting the need to copy someone else's gifts. When you discover your own gifts and no longer feel the need to compete with others, you'll have discovered your own identity.

5. Success is the quickest cure for insecurities. The more you excel in your gifts, the more you'll like yourself. Liking yourself is the first step toward your identity!

No one will be able to compete with you when you are secure in your element. Take the time necessary to **discover your purpose.**

CHAPTER FOUR

WOUNDS CAN CREATE A POOR SELF-IMAGE

AVOID THE LIE THAT YOU ARE NOT WORTHY

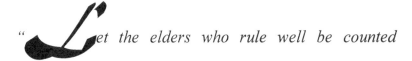

*"**et the elders who rule well be counted*

worthy of double honor, *especially those who labor in the word and doctrine. For the Scripture says, 'You shall not muzzle an ox while it treads out the grain,' and, 'The laborer is worthy of his wages.'"* I Timothy 5:17-18 NKJV

The dictionary describes *"worthy"* as having **worth, value, or merit**.

Since God is your creator, He has placed in you His nature and His image. This alone ascribes worth and value to your life. The proof that you have merit is that you are still here. The fact that you are reading this book is proof that you are worthy. Your waking to a new day is proof that God still sees your greatness and defines your worth. Imagine how many didn't wake to see a new day. Do you realize how many unfinished lives and unfulfilled dreams are lying in the graves of cemeteries all over this world? These are people who failed to realize their worth and assignment and decided to accept their lot in life instead of changing it.

Someone who has been wounded, betrayed or abused by someone they trusted, such as a parent, family member, teacher or babysitter, could be scarred by a mental glitch. Such a person has what I call a hole in their soul, a hole which they have learned to live with over time. Such people learn to cover this hole to help them function in life, but deep within their hearts they have this nagging, burning feeling which shouts, *"What's wrong with me? Why can't I feel and act happy – really happy?"* No matter what they do or accomplish, they assume that they are not worthy of fulfillment. This is insane! If that is you, **stop this insanity today!**

Some churches are misled, teaching that in order to be humble we must believe that we're not worthy. Don't let anyone convince you that humility means being without worth. Christ died so that you could become what you were preordained to be.... **WORTHY!**

Most people who have not yet healed from past hurts and wounds will function under the powerful influences of those wounds. Those who have been hurt by someone in their past begin to believe that they caused that person to hurt them; that they were at fault, deserving the pain. Most of the time this is not true; however, when this thought becomes embedded in their psyche they develop an ideology that they deserve the life they now live. They begin to neglect their dreams and lose their desire to reach for something better or bigger than their own modest existence. Why? The enemy has been knocking them down for so long that they actually believe they belong in the ditch of pain and hurting.

> **YOU WILL NEVER RISE ABOVE YOUR OWN SELF-IMAGE**

When joy tries to enter, they begin to feel guilty. When happiness is knocking on the door of their life, they are afraid to answer because they believe that happiness is reserved for someone else.

Stop accepting your lot in life! Stop making excuses! You are worthy to be healed and to be blessed. You are God's best work! You are created by God, and He can see what you can become when you are healed of your past wounds.

The Bible says that you are fearfully and wonderfully made.

"I will praise thee; for I am fearfully and wonderfully made: marvelous are thy works; and that my soul knoweth right well." Psalm 139:14 KJV

If you keep living under the weight of old lies, you'll not be able to heal. You'll continually treat others the way you perceive and treat yourself. If I'm in relationship with you and you do not feel worthy of my love, then I can't be worthy of your love no matter how hard I try. Your perception of yourself plays an important part in how you receive others and how they receive you. This is not advocating that you should parade your abilities with arrogance and conceit, for that in itself is a sign of unhealed wounds. I'm promoting a healthy view and a liking of your self.

Believe that you are worthy! The Bible verse at the beginning of this chapter says that those who minister are worthy of double honor; that means you are worthy of honor. Confess today that you are worthy of all God's blessings. If those who minister are worthy to receive double honor, then those who do not minister must also be worthy to walk in honor with God.

CHAPTER FIVE

YOU DECIDE YOUR OWN SELF-WORTH

"Self Worth comes from one thing- thinking that you are worthy." Wayne Dyer

"**S**elf-worth" is defined as one's personal worth perceived by oneself.

Building a positive self-portrait is very important for those who have emotional wounds. It paves the way to emotional healing and health. Building a self-portrait means replacing the view of your old or present life with thoughts of healing and success.

*"You will never rise above your **self portrait**..."* Mike Murdock.

A portrait is a painting or reflection of what you or an artist sees. It's not necessarily the truth but what one perceives to be the truth. Someone who has been repeatedly abused, hurt, betrayed, molested and such will develop a false mindset by the portrait that someone else has painted. I assure you that this is not the same picture that God has lovingly designed of you. God sees you not as you are, but as you were destined to be.

God's focus is on the greatness in you and not on the sin or wound you are presently experiencing.

Self -worth is the perception you have of yourself.

Perception means to grasp mentally; to take note of; to observe; to become aware of through sight, hearing, words, touch, taste, or smell.

When you have been fed lies about who you are and

what your value is to life, you'll begin to cultivate misinformation about your self-worth and confidence. This will begin to distort what you see, hear, say, feel, trust, etc. Your whole life becomes a lie. This is exactly where the enemy wants you. He wants to make you feel unimportant, useless, and void of value. Chances are good that what you've accepted as truth is not the truth at all but a false perception.

How much you receive from God depends on your perception of your self-worth. It's easy to live life with the understanding that God is worthy, and with this ideology we offer our gifts to Him. This is good, for we cannot receive a harvest without planting seed. We give with our understanding or perception that what we are giving to is worthy. We plant seed knowing that the soil is good. However, we receive our harvest based on our perception of our self-worth. As long as we are hurt or wounded, believing that we are not worthy to receive good things, our increase and harvest will be hindered. A farmer who believes that he's not deserving of his crop will die poor with abandoned, wasted fields, while all along he could have had ample harvest and much joy. God tries to bless us, but we walk away because we believe that we are not worthy.

I become so frustrated when Christians say, "We are not worthy! We are not worthy of God to save us and to die for us." They may say this with a sincere belief that they must indeed be unworthy. Others may try to humble themselves in light of their failures, believing that the death and resurrection of Jesus is reserved for someone more deserving. The truth is that they are insulting the very reason for Jesus' great sacrifice. God gave His best seed because we are His best creation. We are worthy! We are worthy of all that Heaven has for us, but many will never experience the best of God because they have allowed someone else to influence them negatively. This reinforces the belief that they are not worthy of such a great gift.

A lack of a healthy view of one's *self* builds upon the inability to have a healthy and normal relationship with others. Poor self-worth will create:

1. *Jealousy*
2. *Insecurities*
3. *A sense of doubt as to why someone would really love you.*

> **PERCEIVED INJURY IS AN INJURY THAT NEVER OCCURRED!**

*"When you're a beautiful person on the inside, there is nothing in the world that can change that about you. Jealousy is the result of one's lack of **self**-confidence, **self-worth**, and **self**-acceptance. The Lesson: If you can't accept yourself, then certainly no one else will."* Shasha Azevedo

No one can have a healthy relationship with anyone if they can't trust them. Pure torture is being in love with someone who is not in love with you. This creates a constant unrelenting fear that the person you love must be making a big mistake in loving you, and your heart will always doubt the sincerity of their love. Their absence can overpower you with fear and dread that they are cheating on you. Jealousy is a poison that only you can cure. The venom of jealousy is birthed in the mind of betrayal. A jealous spirit pollutes the mind and deceives the heart. This kind of person will always live in perceived injury.

Perceived injury is an injury that never occurred. You just perceived it. You've conjured it up by your past experiences and pain. Instead of greeting the person you love with open arms, warmth, joy and love, you greet them with distrust, inquisitions, perceived pain and wounds until they've exhausted their means of making you feel okay. The truth is you're not ok! You're wounded and hurt from something or someone in your past. You haven't released it, which keeps you and your love locked behind the prison bars of your falsely perceived injury and jealousy.

Think about it. If your mom and dad didn't treat you right… didn't love or protect you… were never there when you needed them… why would anyone else? The truth is that someone else *can* and *will* love you! You just can't see or receive it because you don't love yourself. You can't see how anyone could possibly love you because you see yourself as unlovable based on your past experiences. I know you try hard to be loved! I know you cry and you toss and turn at night, wondering what is wrong with you. There is nothing wrong with you, but there is something wrong with the perception you have of yourself.

Your mind has believed lies for so long that you are convinced that you're no good. **Come on!** This affects your self-worth, not because your worth has cheapened, not because you're really worthless but because you *believe* that you're worthless. Your false belief has cheapened your life and your relationships, but in God's eyes you are worthy and have never stopped being worthy, regardless of your past. The proof that God still sees you as worthy and still believes in you is that you are still alive.

- *Who told you that you can't change?*
- *Who told you that you were no good?*
- *Who said that you have to keep repeating the same realities?*

If we believe the lie that we have no control over our lives, we'll die. If we can't change, then what's the purpose of the cross, and how do we explain those who have changed? The truth is that we can change! We've been conditioned to believe that what's around us is more important than what is in us. The truth is that when we fix what's inside, we will change what is outside.

If we are not worthy, then why did the Psalmist say that God has crowned man with His glory?

"O LORD, our Lord, how majestic is your name in all the earth! You have set your glory above the heavens. From the lips of children and infants you have ordained praise because of your enemies, to silence the foe and the avenger. When I consider your heavens, the work of your fingers, the moon and the stars, which you have set in place, what is man that you are mindful of him, the son of man that you care for him? You made him a little lower than the heavenly beings and crowned him with glory and honor. You made him ruler over the works of your hands; you put everything under his feet: all flocks

and herds, and the beasts of the field, the birds of the air, and the fish of the sea, all that swim the paths of the seas. O LORD, our Lord, how majestic is your name in all the earth!" Psalm 8:1-9 NIV

Did you see it? What is a man that you have been so mindful of him? If you and I were not worthy, why would God keep His mind on us? If you were no good, why would God make you higher than His created angels? In the Hebrew the phrase *"**a little lower than the heavenly beings"*** is interpreted as 'elohiym' (el-o-heem'); *plural of OT: gods in the ordinary sense; but specifically used (in the plural thus, especially with the article) of the supreme God* (Copyright (c) 1994, Biblesoft and International Bible Translators, Inc.).

What did God crown us with? Not gold, or silver or anything precious. God crowned man with a piece of Himself... with the **GLORY OF GOD!** After God crowned man, He placed him to rule over His works by placing everything under his feet. Would God crown you with His Glory; would He place it within you to give you authority over the rest of creation if you were not worthy? Absolutely not!

Once you understand that your self-worth is not based on others or negative circumstances others have created, you'll understand that God has always had a divine and glorious plan for you. Your self-worth was established before you were even born. That plan is for you to become great for Him.

Your spouse, your friends and those around you will never really determine your self-worth. The only person who determines your worth is **you**. Take God's word and begin to re-sculpture your self-worth. Start today!

CHAPTER SIX

STEPS TO
BUILDING A HEALTHY
SELF CONFIDENCE

"Never bend your head. Always hold it high. Look the world straight in the face." Helen Keller

*"I rejoice therefore that I have **confidence** in you in all things."* 2 Corinthians 7:16 KJV

I love this quote. Here is a person who lived under great infirmities. Helen Keller was deaf, dumb and blind. However, her confidence was not built on her physical weakness, but on her mental ability to realize that her identity was based on what she would become and not on what she was. For Helen Keller to become the woman she became, someone had to mentor her and show her that there was more to her life than just being able to see, hear and speak. If we are to succeed, we are going to have to overlook our weaknesses and begin to build our confidence, believing that there is more to us than just our basic abilities.

Helen Keller challenges us to look the world straight in the face. Don't you think it peculiar that she would brave us to do what she could not do? Maybe she was referring to something greater than physical sight. Helen's "looking" must have involved more than seeing with your eyes. Her sight was deeper than the eyes of her face. She was referring to our inner person. She was telling us to build our confidence, never drop our head as though we're lower than our worth, but always hold it high to see our glorious God-given destiny. Be proud of who you are. No matter what life deals you, you can achieve and succeed.

"One man who has a mind and knows it, can always beat ten men who haven't and don't." George Bernard Shaw

Lack of self-confidence is one of the greatest problems we face in this country. No wonder we've made Hollywood our example. We've made those who drive nice cars, live in big houses and have lots of money the focal point of what we believe to be genuine success. This is not reality. Many of the well-to-do have more heartaches and depression than those who have very little. Material things were never meant to create real happiness. Real success places value on attributes such as honor, integrity, love, God, and a secure and happy home.

Confidence is a belief in your own abilities and talents without comparing yourself with everyone else. When you compare yourself to someone else, you'll always come up short in the comparison because you always compare your weaknesses to the strengths of others.

NEEDY PEOPLE ARE NEVER SATISFIED!

Self-confidence is the key ingredient to a healthy and healed life.

Insecurities, inadequacies, low self-esteem, fear, bitterness, inferiorities and relational hurts can all damage your self-confidence and your hope of a better life. Hope is what faith is built on. Self-confidence leads to self realization and will produce a healthy self-image.

When we lack a good healthy confidence in ourselves, we begin to develop hopelessness and a spirit of "why bother?"

"Why should I try to be better? Why should I take the time to change? I'm no good!" These are thought patterns that need to be dealt with. Why take the time? Because you're better than what you think you are!

Hope is necessary for us to live and survive the rat race of life. Hope is simply a feeling that what is wanted will happen. Hope is desire with expectation. Hope is trust and reliance on what you are hoping for.

BELIEVE IN YOURSELF

Have faith in your own abilities. You cannot be successful or happy if you don't have confidence in your own powers and your own abilities. Many suffer from what is known as an "inferiority complex." I like what Norman Vincent Peale said in his book, *"The Power of Positive Thinking."*

"We must approach the maladies of our emotional life as a physician probes to find something wrong physically."

This cannot be done immediately, certainly not overnight. It may require some counseling. Let me give you a scripture that you need to quote daily; *"I can do all things through Christ which strengthens me"* (Philippians 4:13).

"What you do daily is deciding what you are becoming permanently."

Self confidence is vital for a good and healthy emotional life. When someone is lacking in this area, they tend to become very needy.

NEEDY PEOPLE ARE NEVER SATISFIED

Persons who haven't developed their identity become dependent on others to qualify them in order to feel accepted and needed. This attitude will always exhaust the other person in the relationship. No one is capable of supplying what you need every single day. If you're a person who constantly needs to be told that you're pretty... you're okay... you're successful, you'll reproach those you depend on that do not supply you with the confirmations or compliments you need to feel good about yourself. No human was designed to supply the qualities of another person. That is a job for the Holy Spirit. God designed us to draw our strength, love and acceptance from the Holy Spirit. He's the person who will never leave you. He's the person in your life who understands you and will never expect anything from you that you are unable to supply.

Spend several minutes each day visualizing your success and what you are becoming, not what you are. Learn to build an environment that promotes your confidence. Surround yourself with positive pictures, bible verses or anything encouraging that will help you start believing in yourself.

Your confidence is a feeling. Feelings of confidence depend on the type of thoughts that you constantly let run through your mind.

YOUR MIND IS YOUR WORLD

You will never be able to build a healthy confidence if you don't control your mind. Think defeat and you will be defeated. Think you're not worthy and you will not be worthy. Someone once said, *"If you think you can or you think you can't, your right!"* Start thinking confident thoughts. When you begin to feel confident, you will start to sense a new power surging from your life. Let me stress that focusing on your self-worth must be preceded with focusing on the Lord. Don't attempt any self-focus without first acknowledging the Lord your God. A good self-confidence will aid in building your faith, and faith will recondition your attitude.

Begin to fill your mind with pleasant thoughts throughout your day. Stop feeding your pain. Stop feeding your wound. Allow your pain to create in you a passion to relieve others of their pain. Change your focus. Fill your mind with thoughts of faith, confidence and security. This will begin to expel those negative and defeated thoughts.

Emerson once said, *"They conquer **who think** they can."*

"As he thinks in his heart, so is he." Proverbs 23:7 *NKJV*

YOU MUST FIGHT YOUR FEARS

Fear is the most deadly of all spirits. Fear will paralyze the greatest of men. Fear is the reason so many fail to change because it keeps them in their prison of doubt and low self esteem.

Emerson added to his quote: *"Do the thing you fear and the death of fear is certain."* Let me encourage you that fear will never leave. Fear can only be conquered. For fear to be conquered, it has to be faced. Stop allowing fear to stop your change. Stop allowing fear to control your life. Fear causes you not to step out... not to try. If you never try, you'll never know. I'd rather try and fail than never try at all.

When General Stonewall Jackson was planning an attack during the Civil War, he was outnumbered and the endeavor appeared to be impossible. One of his officers remarked that he feared they would not be able to accomplish the task.

> **"NEVER TAKE COUNSEL OF YOUR FEARS." STONEWALL JACKSON**

General Stonewall's reply to this officer was powerful. He said, *"Never take counsel of your fears."* Once you stop letting fear dominate your thought-life, you'll be able to walk into new areas of life. Your relationships, your marriage and your family life will be better. Happiness will begin to flood your life.

I speak from experience. For years I had such a low self-esteem. My confidence had no teeth. I was easily discouraged. I always needed someone to pump me up... to make me feel important. I was uncomfortable with silence. If I wasn't the center of attention in a room of people I immediately assumed that something was wrong with me. Thank God I've been healed of such pain. I tell you the truth; when you live with fears, low self-esteem, and an unhealthy confidence, your life is a cesspool of anger and bitterness.

PEACEFUL MIND

My spiritual father, Dr. Mike Murdock, said something that I'll never forget. *"Son, follow your peace. Learn to build a life without stress and a nest without thorns."* We were at a hotel room and he had just ended what must have been a rather frustrating telephone conversation. We spent the next hour talking about peace and how we need to have a peaceful mind, a mind that is not cluttered with junk, torture and confusion. Jesus said, *"Peace I leave with you."* His peace!

"Peace I leave with you, my peace I give unto you: not as the world giveth, give I unto you. Let not your heart be troubled, neither let it be afraid. Ye have heard how I said unto you, I go away, and come again unto you. If ye loved me, ye would rejoice, because I said, I go unto the Father: for my Father is greater than I." John 14:27-28 KJV

Satan fears our peace. He fears that when we begin to live a life of peace, our stress and worries will come to an end. The enemy lives on our stress. He feeds on our fears. You must decide if you want a day full of trouble or a mind full of peace. It's your choice. Someone once told me that I should empty my mind nightly before going to bed. That is, in my opinion, only half true. Empty your mind, yes, but if you don't decide to fill it with something better than what was emptied, the enemy will gladly fill it with more junk than you can imagine. For you and me to have a peaceful mind, we have to renew our minds through the Word of God daily.

Let me give you another verse:

"These things I have spoken unto you, that in me ye might have peace. In the world ye shall have tribulation: but be of good cheer; I have overcome the world." John 16:33 KJV

How do we maintain our peace? We must listen to the things Jesus spoke to us about. This Greek word for "peace" is powerful. The Greek word for "peace" is *"eirene" (i-ray'-nay); probably from a primary verb eiro (to join); peace (literally or figuratively); by implication,* **prosperity** (Biblesoft's New Exhaustive Strong's Numbers and Concordance with Expanded Greek-Hebrew Dictionary. Copyright (c) 1994, Biblesoft and International Bible Translators, Inc.).

Can you see why the enemy doesn't want you to have peace? Peace is translated to prosperity. He understands that real peace comes from or originates in Jesus and His words. His peace produces prosperity. When your mind is at rest, you have the ability to create. Your mind is directly attached to your words, and your words are attached to your mind. The thoughts that you think have an effect on what you speak. Thoughts create words. Words are the vehicle of ideas. Words create atmosphere. Words produce attitudes.

SILENCE CAN BE GOLDEN

Ever heard someone say that? Silence is a powerful tool that we have lost, especially in this busy computer and television age. If we're not entertained, we're restless and distracted. Few are able to be quiet or still long enough to experience the joy of silence. A daily practice of silence creates a "peaceful mind."

"Silence is the element in which great things fashion themselves. " Thomas Carlyle

It's in the power of silence that you begin to understand what God is all about. It's in times of quite and stillness that you begin to build within yourself a peaceful environment. Turn off the television, shut the door or go outside and just listen. I promise your life will begin to find meaning.

"Be still, and know that I am God: I will be exalted among the heathen, I will be exalted in the earth." Psalm 46:10 KJV

Let me give you a formula I found, referring to Dr. Norman Vincent Peale:

1. Formulate and stamp onto your mind a mental picture of yourself succeeding.

2. Whenever a negative thought enters your mind, immediately replace it with a positive one.

3. Stop building obstacles in your imagination. When dreaming, dream big... remember it's just a dream.

4. Do not be awestruck by other people and try to copy them.

5. Repeat these dynamic words ten times daily, *"If God is for us, who can be against us?"* (Romans 8:31).

6. Find someone who can mentor you to change.

7. Repeat the following ten times daily, *"I can do all things through Christ who strengthens me."* Philippians 4:13

8. Place yourself in God's hands.

9. Remind yourself that God is with you and that nothing can defeat you.

CHAPTER SEVEN

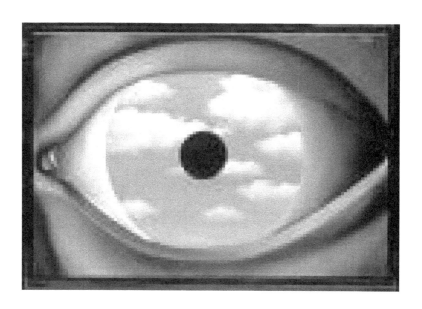

WOUNDS CAN CREATE DISTORTED EMOTIONS

UNDERSTAND THAT YOUR EMOTIONS CAN BE WRONG

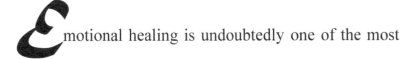

motional healing is undoubtedly one of the most difficult undertakings in life. It is the gateway to evolving a life that is harmonious and fulfilling. It is the antidote to fear.

Where do your wounds come from? They come from your past as you were attempting to learn how to earn love in the face of discovering that you would not always be treated with love or in a loving way.

Love of self, love of God and the love of others are the most important needs of humanity, exceeding by far the physical and material desires which we find ourselves chasing. The importance of the reflexes or responses born of not being loved is that everyone has them in the form of emotional wounds. They are an inevitable consequence of being born into an environment which during our maturing didn't supply us with everything we needed not to be wounded. The truth is that we are all emotionally wounded in some form or fashion. I believe that God allowed all of us to lose something in our childhood that would drive us to seek Him as adults. Although some people are deprived of the necessary need to be loved more than others, we all lack complete wholeness without Jesus.

Many people live their lives never realizing that they have emotional wounds. They assume that friendships and relationships fail due to the faults and problems of others. They cannot envision that they are the linchpin of the many problems surrounding them. Denial or not taking responsibility for one's own problems is a sure sign that emotional wounds are at work. Awareness and receptiveness toward change are necessary for healing to take place.

Look at some of the symptoms of emotional wounds. This is a small list but could you really love someone who repeatedly acted this way? *Anger, fear, hate, depression, sadness, discontent, jealousy, unhappiness, dissatisfaction, helplessness...* and the list goes on.

You may be wondering why such wounds can't heal like any other wounds. The wound that occurs on the external part of your body is exposed to your knowledge; you are aware of how and why the wound was inflicted. This direct knowledge allows you to apply what is necessary to cause healing to take place. Antibiotic ointments, band-aids, crèmes, stitches, etc. are applied soon after the wounding incident. Depending on the size or severity of the wound, you may spend days, weeks or months nurturing and protecting the wound until it is completely healed.

YOU CAN'T FIX WHAT YOU ARE UNWILLING TO FACE.

It is not so with emotional wounds because they are not easily detected and may have evolved over an extended period of time. Many people fail to notice that they've been wounded until they are adults. Emotional wounds occur internally. They are forged in our hearts, minds and souls by others, perhaps someone we've trusted. By the time we realize that we were wounded, we have spent a better part of our life coping and surviving the wound, affecting and infecting many around us. An emotional wound is usually discovered by someone who has been hurt by our wounded behavior. They try to inform us that our actions are not right, that something seems to be very wrong!

HEALING IS ON THE WAY!

I believe that emotional wounds are deep cuts in our soul, mind and psyche. As soon as we recognize the symptoms, we'll understand the value of the cure.

First, locate the wound.

Start searching your heart and past, locate where the wound occurred. This will enable you to face the problem with better knowledge and understanding than when you were first wounded. You may not be able to remember every wound. That is not necessary. When you begin to find and heal one wound, the others may either surface or dissolve in the healing process of the revealed wound. One wound could have created many other wounds; so by healing it, the other wounds can also be healed.

Whatever the wounding process was, go ahead and face it. Perhaps someone spoke hateful words regarding the color of your skin. Go ahead and face it! Consider the person who's hurt you; consider only the human, not his or her race. Attributes, such as race, cannot hurt you. Hurting people hurt people! Forgive them; let them off the hook. Let your heart understand that God and His forgiveness is your reward. God is your shield. No man can determine your destiny; only God and you can. Thus neither people nor race can own or disown you.

How can you know that you have an emotional wound? Start scratching around in your past. If you begin to feel the uncomfortable symptoms of anger, fear or pain in your heart, you are probably hitting a wound. There can be no cure if you are unwilling to find the problem. You can't fix what you are unwilling to face. Locating the wound is facing it. Look at it and command it to come out of the closet of secrecy.

Many people including myself were wounded in their childhood. I speak of it often in my conferences. I wasn't able to learn and read at the pace of others. My inability to learn and read effectively caused many hurts and fears during much of my early life. No matter how many friends I had, I always felt inferior. I spent most of my early life trying to fit in, to somehow feel good enough. I did not begin to heal until I was brave enough to face and unlock my dark and secret closet to God. I could not heal until I was willing to expose the wounds to God and to cry in His presence.

When I was willing to go back to locate the pain, the wound and the fear, I began to feel much better about myself.

I recall being so fearful that I would run from almost all fights. I was constantly picked on by those who were bigger than I was. I would run, hide and do everything I could think of to avoid an encounter with those who picked on me. Imagine trying to survive each new school day, each new school year by constantly dreading and dodging school bullies. What a mess! What a nightmare! I can tell you that these memories hurt even now, but thank God I've got the victory! I've faced the demons of my past and now I am a better person because of it. I encourage you to locate your wound. Your healing is on the way and many times better than anything you've ever tried!

Second, clean the wound.

Cleaning the wound is next. When I clean a physical wound, I remove any dirt or foreign material that is in the wound and apply an antiseptic to kill harmful bacteria. When I clean an emotional wound, I must remove the effects of the event that created the wound. How does this work? The debris in an emotional wound is the emotion I experience when I become wounded. The emotion could be frustration, shock, anger, disappointment, shame. There are many, and they all start with fear.

Cleaning the wound causes the pain of the wound to bleed again. Having to remove debris and dead skin from a wound can be very painful. It means having to face the pain again. You may cry. You may feel all the same emotions you felt when the wound was first inflicted.

I have counseled many who have shut themselves off from feeling any emotion. They ignore the source of their wound and even deny the wound itself to avoid feeling the pain. People usually try to hide their wound so that they never have to look at it again. If they could have responded to the wound immediately, they might have avoided becoming emotionally scarred. Instead, they learn to live with the scar for a very long time.

To remove any negative emotions, I must mentally return to the moment the wound was created. I must revive the emotion, not just remember it – **I must relive it.** I must vent the emotion as I fully experienced it. I challenge you to let the past wound bleed once more. **Let it out!** I promise that you will be on your way to healing.

Third, apply a bandage and allow it to heal and scar properly.

Your emotional wound needs to be protected while it heals. The bandage for emotional wounds is *compassion.* You must have compassion for whoever wounded you. Compassion is birthed when you recognize that whoever wounded you is probably wounded themselves. Go ahead and forgive the people who hurt you. I know that this seems hard to do, but I promise that your healing waits at the end of forgiveness.

A scar is a sign that a wound was once present. Don't despise your scars. They are the proof you've survived your crisis. Use God's Word as the bandage. Wrap yourself in the arms of God. Allow the Holy Spirit to become the "Balm of Gilead." Let His oil of love, peace and acceptance spill on your wound to cause healing.

Some wounds may not be cured, only relieved. A cure is the elimination of the causes of symptoms, not just the relief. Some wounds may never be completely eliminated. Some wounds are necessary for you to succeed in life. This is not to say that a wound should keep controlling you, but that you learn to control the wound. Your wound may be the very womb from which your future will be birthed. All you need to do is face the wound, and God will do the birthing. Your wound might be turning into your womb as you are reading these words right now. God could be preparing your wound to birth your greatness this very moment.

YOU CAN'T FIX WHAT YOU'RE UNWILLING TO FACE.

When people are wounded, abused or abandoned at an early age, they tend to build walls around their wounds to mentally shut them away to be lost forever. The problem with this is that the wound they believe is gone is increasingly controlling them.

The enemy has power over your wound or pain as long as you keep your secret closet sealed, and he will expose it at the most improper moments for the rest of your life. No matter how much you believe it's gone, it will surface over and over again.

I once had one of those closets. I shut that closet, locked it up tight and threw away the key. Every time I entered my secret place to pray, God would nudge me to release what was in my closet. Once during prayer, as God was prodding me once more about my secret closet, I reacted with much anger and hurt. I explained to God that what was in that closet was over and done, and that no one needed to ever know about it!

The Lord replied in a still small voice, *"Son, unless you face what's in the closet of your past, it will inevitably destroy you."* It is the same with you and your secret closet. You can't fix the pains of your past or their negative influences in your life if you can't even face them. If your past pains have your attention, they are still controlling you.

No matter how painful it is, be brave. Go ahead and open that closet. Air it out in front of the Lord. Do it! Don't let what's been hurting you stay even one more night in your heart. Open the door. Let it GO! It's over!

ANYTHING UNCONTESTED WILL FLOURISH!

Uncontested means that you will not oppose it.

I have learned that you can't change or fix anything you tolerate. I use to tolerate my wound, my pains and my hurts. Now I face them so I can fix them. What you tolerate continues to grow.

Someone once told me that conduct permitted is conduct taught. That also goes for what you allow the wound to do to you. Your toleration is giving your wound a foundation to build a prison you will never get out of. Go ahead and face each block of your walls of pain and hurt. Tell them they don't hurt you anymore and watch the walls come tumbling down!

CHAPTER EIGHT

YOUR MIND IS YOUR WORLD

"What the mind can conceive and believe it can achieve." Napoleon Hill

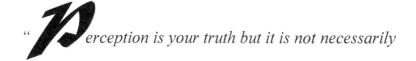

*"**P**erception is your truth but it is not necessarily the truth."* Dr. Jerry Grillo

Perception is the power of your own reality. What someone perceives can be stronger than what is really true. You have probably built a system of false truths by your perceptions if you've spent your life in wounds and hurt feelings.

Wounded people look through a stained-glass window that has been colored by their perception. You need to allow the Holy Spirit to come in and change your window. When you look through a stained-glass window, the images on the other side are distorted; the depth perception has changed. The image is either bigger or smaller than it really is.

This is exactly what happens to people who have been stained by wounds of their past. Their perception has become so distorted that they see and judge everything through their stained-glass window of emotions. Every facet of life has been altered by their false perceptions.

Truth is distorted when perception is distorted.

Imagine how heartbreaking it would be to one day face Jesus and find that your whole life was nothing but a lie. God warned you not to let your perceptions deceive you, not to let them cost you the blessings that He had reserved for you. Don't let such a tragedy become your story. Remember that your emotions are not always telling the truth. Emotions are what you are feeling. If you are feeling what your wounds have created in your past, then your perception of those feelings is false. Why? Your perception has become distorted over time and is now interpreting the feelings of your present. Please realize that past feelings may not change overnight. You have to control your emotions when they speak wrong thoughts to you. If you do not control your emotions, your emotions will control you.

Your mind is your world.

Your mind creates your emotions. Your mind controls your feelings. Your mind is your world. Remember, you will never outperform your own self-image. Your self-image is a direct result of what your mind keeps hearing. What you keep

> **EVERYTHING YOU DO IS IN SEARCH OF A FEELING!**

hearing you will eventually believe. If someone you trusted repeatedly tells you *that you're stupid...you will never amount to anything... you're ugly...you're no good...* you will eventually believe it to be the truth.

Your mind is the key to what you believe. If negative words are constantly hurled at you, they will eventually condition your mind to believe that they are indeed true words. Over time, a lie becomes the truth. Imagine living half of your life hearing wrong words. By the time you are an adult, you've been conditioned to believe that what you've heard is the truth. Can you see how damaging this is? You can be saved and serving the

Kingdom, submitted to the Spirit's calling, but you will never fully possess all that God has destined for your life until you allow God to expose and heal all of your past wounds. This process begins in your mind.

The dictionary defines "mind" as "M*emory; recollection or remembrance (to bring to mind...) what one thinks; opinion. That which thinks, perceives, feels, wills, etc.; Seat or subject of consciousness, the thinking and perceiving part of consciousness; intellect or intelligence, attention; notice, all of an individual's conscious and the unconscious together as a unit* (©1995 Zane Publishing, Inc. ©1994, 1991, 1988 Simon & Schuster, Inc.).

"And be not conformed to this world: but be ye transformed by the renewing of your mind, that ye may prove what is that good, and acceptable, and perfect, will of God." Romans 12:2 KJV

"That ye be not soon shaken in mind, or be troubled, neither by spirit, nor by word, nor by letter as from us, as that is the day of Christ at hand." 2 Thessalonians 2:2 KJV

Everything we do, we do in search of a feeling.

Remember your feelings can be wrong. What you're feeling could be a lie. If you are not grounded in the reality of who you really are, you will always have to battle the feeling that you are no good. People who haven't discovered their purpose are always in competition with those around them. Your feelings are definitely deceiving you if what God is doing in your life never seems good enough.

Stop listening to the voice of your insecurity!

Memories don't die; they must be replaced.

If you want to stop hurting, start changing your memories. Replace them with present memories of victory and accomplishments no matter how small they seem. Look around you and discover the things that are worthy of your praise and begin to focus on them. Focus creates blindness. When you are focused on the good around you, you will become blind to the pain that is in your past.

Develop a grateful heart. Thankfulness replenishes the atmosphere where miracles can grow. You could be dead right now. Your life could have ended in your past. Thank God it didn't. Wholeness comes from thankfulness.

The fastest way to overcome emotional wounds and feelings is to have an encounter with God. He is much greater than the wound itself.

"And he fell to the earth, and heard a voice saying unto him, Saul, Saul, why persecutest thou me? And he said, Who art thou, Lord? And the Lord said I am Jesus whom thou persecutest: it is hard for thee to kick against the pricks." Acts 9:4-5 KJV

Saul was changed that day! His passion was redirected to serving Jesus, the very person he was persecuting. What changed him? He had an encounter with something much greater than his past. We all have a mental picture of who we think we are, how we look, what we're good at and what our weaknesses might be. We develop this picture over time, starting when we were very young. The term "**self-image**" is used to refer to a person's "mental picture" of him or herself. A lot of our self-image is based on our interactions with other people as well as life's experiences. This mental picture (our self-image) contributes to our **self-esteem**.

Self-esteem is all about how much we *feel valued, loved, accepted* and *thought well of* by others — and how much we *value, love,* and *accept ourselves.* People with healthy self-esteem are able to feel good about themselves and appreciate their own worth. They take pride in their abilities, skills, and accomplishments. People with low self-esteem may feel as if no one will ever like or accept them, or they may feel that they can't succeed in anything.

Self-Esteem Problems

Before people can overcome self-esteem problems and build a healthy sense of worth, they need to recognize what might be causing those problems in the first place. Two things in particular can have a big impact on our self-esteem: 1) how others see or treat us, and 2) how we see ourselves.

Self-esteem can be damaged when someone whose opinion we value (be it a parent, teacher, or friend) repeatedly put us down. It creates in us an echoing voice that becomes our inner critic, building in us a low self-esteem.

Unrealistic expectations can also affect a person's self-esteem. People have an image of who they want to be or who they think they should be. Everyone's image of the ideal person is different. For example, some people admire athletic skills while others admire academic abilities. People who see themselves as having the qualities they admire — such as the ability to make friends easily — usually have high self-esteem. People who don't see themselves as having the qualities they admire may develop low self-esteem. Unfortunately, people who have low self-esteem often *do* have the qualities they admire, they just can't see it.

Why Is Self-Esteem Important?

How we feel about ourselves can influence how we live our lives. People who feel they are accepted by others usually have better relationships. They are more likely to ask for help and support from friends and family. People who believe they can accomplish goals and solve problems are more likely to do well in school. A good self-esteem allows you to accept yourself and live life to the fullest.

Your mind paints certain pictures of things in your present by using the colors of your past. Whoever was in charge of holding the paint brush in your past determines what the pictures of your present will look like. If someone you trusted used disturbing colors to paint your life's story, then what should have been brushstrokes of self-worth, self-esteem, self-confidence and security really became disfigured marks creating a false picture of your true self. You must allow the Master Painter to repaint your life to what is true, pure, and right.

We've all had some wrong pictures painted; some more colorful than others, some more intensely distorted or disturbing than others. The truth of the matter is that we are all victims of our minds. We have all experienced problems with low self-esteem at certain times in our lives — especially during teen years as we tried to discover who we are. The good news is that you can change your self-image by changing the way you think about yourself.

"Finally, brethren, whatsoever things are true, whatsoever things are honest, whatsoever things are just, whatsoever things are pure, whatsoever things are lovely, whatsoever things are of good report; if there be any virtue, and if there be any praise, think on these things." Philippians 4:8 KJV

We all have to take control of our thoughts. Your world is what you think. Your self-worth, your feelings and your joy all live within the boundaries of your mind. YOUR MIND IS YOUR WORLD.

STEPS TO IMPROVING SELF-ESTEEM:

- **Stop thinking negative thoughts about yourself.** Instead of focusing on your shortcomings, start concentrating on your good qualities. When you catch yourself being too critical of yourself, counter it with your positive traits. Each day write down three things about yourself that make you happy.

- **Aim for accomplishments rather than perfection.** Attempting to attain perfection will paralyze you, but accomplishments, no matter the size, will give you the confidence needed to take that next step.

- **View mistakes as learning opportunities.** Accept the fact that you will make mistakes — everyone does. Mistakes are part of learning. Remind yourself that your talents are constantly developing. Everyone excels at different rates, accomplishing different things; that's what makes people interesting.

- **Try new things.** How will you ever discover your strengths if you don't try something new?

- **Recognize what you can change and what you can't.** Take courage to change the things you're capable of changing. Utilize God's help to do your best, and leave the rest in His care.

- **Set goals.** Each goal achieved adds another brick toward building your self-worth.

- **Take pride in your opinions and ideas.** Don't be afraid to voice them.

- **Exercise!** You will relieve stress and become healthier as well as happier.

- **Have fun!**

Self-esteem plays a role in almost everything you do. People with high self-esteem do better in school and find it easier to make friends. They tend to have better relationships with peers and adults, feel happier, and find it easier to deal with mistakes, disappointments, and failures. This enables them to pursue something until they succeed. It takes some work, but it's a skill they'll have for life.

The only freedom you have is to be yourself!

CHAPTER NINE

THE DIFFERENCE
IN PEOPLE IS
WHAT THEY SEE

"If you change the way you look at things, the things you look at will change." Wayne Dyer

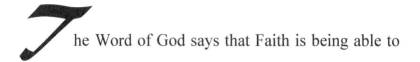

he Word of God says that Faith is being able to

believe what you are unable to see. God's Word teaches us, *"Now faith is the substance of things hoped for, the evidence of things not seen....."* (Hebrews 11:1 KJV) Have faith in your own life. Have faith that you are going to become emotionally healed and set free today. I can't imagine living life without the ability to change the way I see things. Go ahead, give it a try!

Take another look! Could it be that all you need to do is change the way you've been conditioned to see?

ANSWERING THE QUESTION OF LIFE

Who am I? Where do I come from? What is the reason for my existence? What am I expected to do? Where am I going? All these questions are being birthed in the mind. The answer is clear. Yes, you are here for a reason. You were created to do something for God. Let's understand this one basic fact. God is the Creator and you are His creation. Would a creator create something without plan or purpose? NO!

God created you for a reason. God created you with a plan and a purpose. *"For I know the plans I have for you," declares the LORD, "plans to prosper you and not to harm you, plans to give you hope and a future."* *(Jeremiah 29:11 NIV)*

Failure to use the power of thought is the reason most of

us are in bondage. There is power in your thoughts. We become limited when we don't allow our minds to be stretched beyond what we see. What we are looking at is not necessarily real. You will repeat the same mistakes when you are in bondage to your thought life.

Why do people repeat the same reality?

Why do people choose the same relationships?

Why do people get the same jobs over and over again?

We've become conditioned to our daily lives. We've bought into the crazy idea that we have little or no control to change what needs changing. We've been conditioned to believe that our external world is more substantial and real than our internal world. We only believe what we can see to be true, rather than believing and trusting that there is more than meets the eye. Circumstances around us create realities within us. Our brain does not know the difference between what it sees and what is real. The brain holds the power of thought and imagination. The brain constructs its own reality from what it perceives or receives. The power of seeing lies in what you believe you see.

WE DON'T HAVE TO KEEP RELIVING THE SAME MISTAKES!

What is real? What is reality? These questions have been asked in our churches for so long that no one seems to know the answer anymore. Is what I see, feel and believe reality? Was the rock only there because I felt it as I kicked it? Is my pain proof that the rock is real? Is reality limited to what I see and feel? We've been conditioned to believe that matter is more important than space. We are people of matter. The truth is that God doesn't live in matter; He lives in space. There is much more space than there is matter. Consider the room you are occupying. What do you see; a chair, a couch, maybe a desk or a bed? What surrounds you is matter. Yet around all that matter is space. Now look again. Unless you are the ultimate pack-rat, there should be more space than matter. Even if your room was packed to the ceiling with matter, space would still abound because it is not confined to your room.

If God lives in space, then there is more of God in your life than you can perceive. To see matter you have to look through space. You have to look through God's dimension to see matter, to see your desk for instance. Now what if you could see into the other dimension? What if, for a brief moment, God allowed you to look into the space you occupy instead of looking through it? Don't think this can't happen? It happens all the time.

I've heard that your eyes feed your brain 400 billion bits of information per second, yet your mind will only process 2,000 bits per second. This gets my curiosity. If your mind receives 400 billion bits of information, but processes only 2,000, what are you missing?

What then does the *seeing*... the eyes or the brain? According to the above statement, the eyes have no objective. They are like lenses on a camera. They receive or gather everything they point at. So, if our eyes have no objective, it seems safe to assume that our eyes really don't see. It's our minds that see. If our minds are not conditioned to believe certain things, then our minds will not reveal what they don't believe to be real. The only thing that our minds will reveal is that which pertains to our world, environment or life. Our reality is restricted to our own limited dimension. The mind has to be reconditioned to believe that there is more than what is confined within its own space, time zone, environment, likes and dislikes.

Could we see more if we believed more? There must be more to our world than what we see. Let us recondition our minds to see **beyond ourselves.**

"While we look not at the things which are seen, but at the things which are not seen: for the things which are seen are temporal; but the things which are not seen are eternal." 2 Corinthians 4:18 KJV

"But as it is written, Eye hath not seen, nor ear heard, neither have entered into the heart of man, the things which God hath prepared for them that love him. But God hath revealed them unto us by his Spirit: for the Spirit searcheth all things, yea, the deep things of God." 1 Corinthians 2:9-10 KJV

Faith is the ability to see that which is unseen. Faith believes something before it can be seen. Your natural eyes may see your cancer, yet your spiritual eye sees or believes in its healing.

Your eyes see your pain. Your eyes see a messed up relationship. Your eyes see what your faith believes not to be true. HAVE FAITH AND TAKE ANOTHER

LOOK!

Look at your life through the lenses of faith. Instead of seeing what was, start seeing what could be. Your life suddenly looks better than it ever has. Your home looks better! Your relationship looks better! Your finances look better!

Trust me; this is your time for a harvest of change and greatness.

Here is another example of the Bible that fully explains how one can suddenly see with a different mindset:

"And when the servant of the man of God was risen early, and gone forth, behold, an host compassed the city both with horses and chariots. And his servant said unto him, Alas, my master! How shall we do? And he answered, Fear not: for they that be with us are more than they that be with them. And Elisha prayed, and said, LORD, I pray thee, open his eyes, that he may see. And the LORD opened the eyes of the young man; and he saw: and, behold, the mountain was full of horses and chariots of fire round about Elisha." 2 Kings 6:15-17 KJV

Wasn't the army of the Lord there all the time? Why didn't the servant see it before the prophet told him to look again?

Could it be that the servant saw the Lord's horse all along? His brain refused to reveal what his eyes perceived, creating a misled reality based on only parts of the picture.

Then Elisha prayed for the Lord to open his eyes that he might see. We know that the servant wasn't blind. Or was he? Was he blind to the miracle? Did his lack of faith stop him from seeing? Is yours?

Stop looking at what you think is real, and start looking at your life again. God is trying to reveal the whole truth to you.

AGAIN, TAKE ANOTHER LOOK!

CHAPTER TEN

TRUST ISN'T A FEELING
TRUST IS A DECISION

"Trust is the ability to ask and believe even after you have been disappointed" Dr. Jerry Grillo

*F*irst of all, I'm not suggesting that everyone should be trusted, but past wounds create the tendency not to trust anyone.

People tend to protect themselves from further pain as long as past wounds have not healed properly. The fear of being hurt again will create distrust and keep others at a distance.

An open wound of distrust leaks its poison into every relationship. Such poison keeps any relationship from growing and maturing to the next level. When a relationship stops maturing, it stagnates. It's in the stagnated season that most relational wars begin. These wars usually end up in separation… whether it is divorce, a broken friendship, or a parent and child at odds with each other.

This sense of distrust builds a wall of defense. Such a wall is meant to keep the wounded person protected and safe from further harm. In reality nothing good can get in and nothing bad can escape. Expulsion is as necessary as addition. Any mature and healthy relationship operates under a *give and take* principle. If both have walls, neither can give nor receive. Often times, one partner tries to do all the giving while starving for attention.

Trust is a firm belief and confidence in the honesty, integrity, reliability and justice of a person. Start believing in the good of people. Find one thing about someone you like and begin to build on that quality. Remember, I don't mean that you should trust everybody. It's obvious that we can't trust everybody, but that doesn't mean we can't trust somebody.

To be able to adopt a different perspective, you'll have to trust the person God has assigned over you.

TRUST IS A DECISION

TRUST IS NOT EARNED

Many who have been betrayed by those they've trusted, such as family members or authority figures, find it impossible to trust anyone else again. Rightfully so, their sense of security and safety have been betrayed and shattered. They've been badly hurt by those they've trusted. Why risk trusting anyone again, even if some intend no harm?

Trust is the firm belief and confidence in ones integrity, honesty, reliability and justice toward another person. Someone who's been hurt in the past will build a wall of perceived protection. Remember the story of the woman at the well? She lived in Samaria, the city of Sychar. Samaria means "a hedge with thorns." Over time, hurting people acquire the skills necessary to trim their hedges of pain and distrust, making them presentable. Wounded people survive life by masking their pain and hurt, which causes others to assume that they are okay. In the case of the Samaritan woman, there was no trust. Anyone who gets too close to someone wounded will be pricked by the hidden thorns of the well-trimmed hedges of past hurts and pains.

"Now Jericho was securely shut up because of the children of Israel; none went out, and none came in." Joshua 6:1 NKJV

Jericho represented security, hiding behind the walls of presumed safety. Jericho was tightly shut up. Nothing could get in but nothing could get out either. Relationships are a two-way street. If you are so tightly guarded that nothing and no one can get in, then guess what? Nothing you do can get out either. You are a fortified city full of pain and hurt; no healing can enter and no pain can escape. You become so accustomed to the pain – it's been your predictable accomplice for so long – that you fear you can't survive without it. This is absurd. You can't trust your pains more than people! You must learn to trust again. Not everyone in your life is going to hurt you.

VICTIM OR VICTOR...IT'S YOUR CHOICE. There are certain things that you have no control over. You couldn't choose your race. You couldn't pick the parents of your preference. You were given no choice as to how much love and nurturing you would receive as a child. You couldn't select the information you wished to learn in your first five years of life. It is suggested that eighty percent of what we learn by the age of five will help determine who we are.

> **STOP LIVING IN YOUR PAST AND START LEARNING FROM IT!**

The first part of your life was not in your control, which made you vulnerable to being hurt. You became an unsuspecting victim, but now you are an adult! You've been freed from the chains of childhood. Many adults are still being controlled by the inner victim or child. It survives by feeding on distrust, fear, and insecurities; but the child must grow up. Your inner child must yield its life to the adult you're trying to become so that you can stop being a victim and start living victorious!

YOU HAVE THE VICTORY! *"But thanks be to God, which giveth us the victory through our Lord Jesus Christ. Therefore, my beloved brethren, be ye stedfast, unmoveable, always abounding in the work of the Lord, forasmuch as ye know that your labour is not in vain in the Lord."* 1 Corinthians 15:57-58 KJV

"O sing unto the LORD a new song; for he hath done marvelous things: his right hand, and his holy arm, hath gotten him the victory." Psalm 98:1 KJV

"For whatsoever is born of God overcometh the world: and this is the victory that overcometh the world, even our faith. Who is he that overcometh the world..." 1 John 5:4-5 KJV

You have the victory through the blood of Jesus. He conquered suffering and death to help us conquer our past pain and hurt. Take control of your life, perhaps for the first time ever. Don't let the bullies of your past rob you of a healthy and fulfilling future. Let trust grow again.

LET ME GIVE YOU A TRUST LIST:

1. **Trust in the Lord...** (Proverbs 3:5 NKJV)
2. **Trust in yourself...**
3. **Trust in others...**

Promotion comes to those who are overqualified in their present season...

CHAPTER ELEVEN

LET IT GO AND FORGIVE!

"When you hold resentment toward another, you are bound to that person or condition by an emotional link that is stronger than steel. Forgiveness is the only way to dissolve that link and get free."
Catherine Ponder

*S*omeone once said that when you forgive, you set someone free. The person that becomes liberated is you.

When we refuse to forgive, we are in a sense telling God to move over and let us handle our problems our way. How can we expect God to forgive us if we refuse to forgive others? Even Jesus forgave all who falsely accused and abused Him.

If Jesus can forgive, so can we. Remember that Jesus had the power to call thousands upon thousands of angels to rescue Him at any point during His agony. Jesus never gave up, and at the pinnacle of His pain, His words revealed His spirit:

"Father, forgive them, for they know not what they are doing." Luke 23:34 NIV

Forgiving the one who hurt you isn't in favor of your abuser, but for your release and healing. You are the one who benefits from forgiving someone. When you forgive, you are releasing the power of the infraction; you are freeing yourself from the negative, destructive control it has over you. The quickest way to cure an emotional wound is to forgive the people and things that have caused the wound. Trust me!

THREE AREAS OF FORGIVENESS:

1. Forgive those who have hurt you.

2. Forgive those around you.
3. Forgive yourself.

You're probably thinking, "What did I do?" Nothing! We often blame ourselves when we've been abused, molested or hurt. The hardest person you will have to forgive will be yourself, but go ahead and try it. Lay your hand over your heart and say, "I forgive myself and I release in myself the power of healing in Jesus Name!"

Let me share a story with you.

A person in my congregation was raised under very harsh conditions. His mother was considered partially retarded, and his father was a mean, abusive, and neglectful man.

> **BITTERNESS IS THE POISON YOU'VE CHOSEN TO SWALLOW WHILE WAITING FOR SOMEONE ELSE TO DIE!**

His father would often leave him and his sister in destitute conditions with their mother who could barely take care of herself. He would leave them for weeks, if not months in a one-room apartment, which was so horribly rundown that rainwater would flood the floor for days.

The feeble mother died when the son was only fifteen years old. This left him and his sister to the dreadful whims of their father, who had molested several local children in the community.

This son is now a husband and father of his own. He has grown to be a great father and faithful husband. He lives a meaningful life and has wonderful children and grandchildren as well. I asked him why he seems not to have any scars or dysfunctions from having endured such an abusive childhood, while his sister continually shows signs of abuse such as relational dysfunctions and having been married four times.

His answer was almost too simple; **"I forgave him."**

I had anticipated much more and puzzlingly asked, "Your answer is one phrase?"

To which He replied, "Yes! That's it." The one thing that sets him apart from his sister is forgiveness! He had decided to forgive his father at an early age, which freed him from the ugliness of his past.

Forgiveness doesn't mean accepting the wrongness, but releasing it along with its pain-inflicting power. Let go of the thorn bush if you want to be rid of the thorns and the pain they inflict. Forgiving others doesn't mean having to spend time with them. It just means releasing them along with the harm they've caused. It means untying the ugly knot and freeing your spirit.

UNFORGIVENESS PRODUCES BITTERNESS

Bitterness is the offspring of an unforgiving heart. Bitterness is the poison you've chosen to swallow while you wait for the person who hurt you to die.

Bitterness does not go away; it must be sent away. You will remain bitter as long as you decide to carry the wound. Instead, let it go; let it heal. Bitterness goes when you release it and decide to let it go.

"Let all bitterness, and wrath, and anger, and clamour, and evil speaking, be put away from you, with all malice: And be ye kind one to another, tenderhearted, forgiving one another, even as God for Christ's sake hath forgiven you." Ephesians 4:31-5:1 KJV

The Bible is clear. *Let all bitterness be put away from you.* Who then controls the wound? You do! You must put your bitterness away by being kind and tenderhearted. An act of kindness will begin to melt the frozen heart of hurt and pain.

Bitterness is an obsession to an offense. Bitterness often enters our lives through disappointments, wounds, loss, family trouble, real or perceived injuries, or betrayal.

Bitterness is a root from which other wounds are birthed; *"lest any root of bitterness springing up trouble you, and thereby many be defiled."* Hebrews 12:15

I was painfully pricked by the Holy Spirit one night while watching Christian television because I had hurriedly changed channels to avoid a certain young preacher. The Holy Spirit asked me, "Why do you always change the station as soon as this person comes on?" This question felt like an electric jolt.

My retort was, "He's younger than I am and couldn't possibly have anything to say that I don't already know."

The Holy Spirit responded, "That's not true. You're bitter! You're bitter because you believe that you should have accomplished more by now. You resent his accomplishments because he is so much younger than you are."

Gripped by anger I cried, "That's not true!"

His comeback was calm yet stern, **"SON, YOU'RE BITTER, AND YOU DON'T EVEN KNOW IT!"**

As the truth pierced my heart, I fell prostrate to the floor and repented. My heart was heavy, but as soon as I began to release my hurt and my anger, as soon as I released my bitterness I noticed a heavy burden being lifted from my chest and shoulders. I have since been able to watch this young preacher and extract from him each piece of wisdom that God has placed in him without a trace of bitterness.

Bitterness is a tool the enemy uses to destroy you. It's possible to be bitter without realizing it. Refusing to take the time to take an honest inventory could cost you dearly! Learn to identify the truths about your life.

Stop making excuses about your life; change it.

HOW DOES BITTERNESS ENTER YOUR LIFE?

- *When you believe someone has been unfair to you.*

- *When you've been disrespected by those you are in relationship with.*

- *When someone else is succeeding and you are not.*

- *When you have yet to understand your assignment and significance.*

- *When someone you love succeeds where you have failed.*

- *When you become jealous or envious toward a family member.*

- *When your weaknesses or failures are exposed.*

- *When the love and affection you crave is not given.*

- *Unexplained losses or pain.*

Seeds of bitterness are planted in us daily. We must take up defense in this battle and stop bitterness before it finds root in our hearts and destroys us.

WE MUST CONQUER BITTERNESS

What you fail to conquer will eventually conquer you! Bitterness is the result of a painful memory you haven't yet released. It could have been a father's strict and unemotional love, a spouse's betrayal, a loved one's painful actions, or maybe a painful word spoken to you in your past. All these seeds of bitterness could have caused the wound that is now in dire need of a touch from God. However bitterness finds you, its effects are deadly if not conquered.

DEVASTATING EFFECTS OF BITTERNESS:

- *Bitterness will sever your relationship with God.*

- *Bitterness will destroy all progress in your divine assignment.*

- *Bitterness will confuse your understanding.*

- *Bitterness can birth seasons of curses in your life.*

- *Bitterness will drive your loved ones away from you.*

- *Bitterness can stop the blessings and favor of God.*

- *Bitterness will eventually destroy your relationship with others.*

- *Bitterness will draw satanic attack on your life.*

- *Bitterness can cause you to become a stumbling block to others.*

- *Bitterness will hinder your faith.*

- *Bitterness will cause God not to hear your prayers. When God no longer hears your prayers, Satan no longer heeds your rebukes.*

- *Bitterness can divide your home and destroy your family.*

- *Bitterness can become a generational curse.*

- *Bitterness will send you to hell.*

- *Bitterness causes you to compare your life with those around you.*

- *Bitterness stops access.*

- *Bitterness stops the flow of love.*

"The offense that becomes your obsession destroys your future." Dr. Mike Murdock

God will never use anyone who is bitter. After freeing His children from bondage, and after performing the miracle of the Red Sea, God took His people to the pool of bitter waters. Before God could take His children into the wilderness of mentorship and training, He had to first deal with their bitterness. How did God do this? He turned the bitter waters sweet. God understands that any bitterness not dealt with will keep you from His promise by robbing you of valuable time, as you talk relentlessly about your pain. Whenever the children of Israel talked about Egypt, cancerous bitterness would develop in their hearts. Such bitterness is very costly. Bitterness can cause spiritual abortion. Bitterness will sabotage the plans that God has for your life.

PROOFS OF BITTERNESS:

1. You might be bitter if your desire to retaliate is stronger than the desire to forgive.

2. You might be bitter if you're always sarcastic toward the dreams and goals of others.

3. You might be bitter if you're always magnifying the failures of others above their success.

4. You might be bitter if you're jealous or envious of someone else.

5. You might be bitter if you invest more time explaining your pain than planning your future.

6. You might be bitter if you hate someone who has not harmed you.

7. You might be bitter if you always need to talk about someone. If you can't speak well about someone don't speak at all.

8. You might be bitter if the mention of a certain person or his/her presence immediately affects your countenance.

KEYS TO OVERCOMING BITTERNESS:

Instead of reinventing the wheel let me list Dr. Mike Murdock's keys to overcoming bitterness:

1. *Admit that your heart harbors bitterness.*

2. *Admit your own mistakes.*

3. *Admit that bitterness is robbing you of your joy.*

4. *Stop discussing your pain with those who can't resolve it.*

5. *Stay connected to God's love.*

6. *Meditate on God's Word.*

7. *Stop looking at where you have been, and start looking at where you are going.*

8. *Pray for those who have hurt you.*

9. *Forgive those who have hurt you.*

10. *Forgive yourself!*

11. *Do not seek revenge.*

12. *Ask the Holy Spirit to reveal any hidden sin in your heart.*

13. *Build an expectation for your future.*

You will never have a productive life or relationship if you are living a bitter life. Fight the seeds of bitterness and dig up any past seeds. Allow the love of God to flow over your life today.

Free yourself from the chains of bitterness and un-forgiveness.

FORGIVENESS IS THE QUICKEST CURE FOR EMOTIONAL WOUNDS.

CHAPTER TWELVE

RECEIVE GOD'S LOVE

YOU CAN BE LOVED IF YOU ACCEPT LOVE

*T*here is a big difference between believing that

God loves you and accepting His love. Attending service is easy. Hearing a good gospel message is easy. Really accepting God's love takes faith and effort, especially if you have no nurturing earthly love to compare it to.

Believing in God's love and receiving it are two totally different concepts. You may have a hard time **accepting** love from God if you have been abused, sexually molested, or abandoned by your own parents, grandparents or guardians. You're going to have a difficult time referring to Him as your heavenly Father if you were hurt by your earthly father. How can an abused mind comprehend that God, who is our spiritual Father or parent, be any different?

The truth is that God is not a man. God is not capable of doing the opposite of what He says. He is the truth and all truth is God! Below are some scriptures about what God says about you and His love for you.

"...I will never leave you nor forsake you..." Hebrews 13:5 NKJV

"However, the LORD your God would not listen to Balaam but turned the curse into a blessing for you, because the LORD your God loves you." Deuteronomy 23:5 NIV

"...Because the LORD loved you..." Deuteronomy 7:8 KJV

You will never be totally healed until you accept the love of God. Why not do it right now? You'll begin to love others properly. Before you can love, you have to accept that you are worthy to be loved.

BEGIN TO LOVE YOURSELF

"The entire law is summed up in a single command: 'Love your neighbor as yourself. If you keep on biting and devouring each other, watch out or you will be destroyed by each other. '" Galatians 5:14-15 NIV

The phrase, *"Love your neighbor as yourself,"* occurs over ten times throughout the Scriptures. However, until you love yourself, you will not be able to love anyone or anything correctly. I'm not referring to prideful or hurtful love, which is birthed from selfishness and conceit, but genuinely loving yourself and acknowledging and appreciating your gifts and assignment.

> **WITHOUT A PAST YOUR PRESENT WOULD HAVE NO MEANING!**

You must begin to love what God has made. You're probably saying, "But Bishop, you have no idea how I was treated in my past. If I am so loveable, then why have I been abused, hurt, betrayed, molested?" Take courage knowing that just because someone in your past did not recognize the greatness of God in you, doesn't mean that you are any less than wonderful. You cannot allow people of your past to rule your present, robbing you of your future. I'm not trivializing the fact that you've been hurt, but let the truth be known; you've already survived your past. You are still breathing. You're a conqueror. ***Without your past, your present has no meaning!***

Whatever it is… whoever it was… let it go! You have to learn to love yourself. You can't fully love God if you can't love what He has made. He's made you; *"You are fearfully and wonderfully made"* (Ps 139:14).

- Stop hating yourself.
- Stop hating your past.
- Stop hating others.

Stop letting what others did to you control how you feel about yourself. You are God's handiwork. God is going to use what you've survived. Fall in love with God and His creation, including you. You'll be able to fall in love with others when you do.

The greatest freedom you are ever going to experience is when you receive God's love and forgiveness. When you are receiving God's forgiveness, make sure you forgive your own flaws and failures.

Everybody fails. Everybody has made mistakes. You and I are no different. We must understand that just because someone has hurt us doesn't mean we are the one to blame. Sometimes we hold on to the punishment of a failure because bad feelings are better than no feelings. What you need to do is let it GO! Let yourself be free. Free your mind and free your past. You have the rest of your life ahead of you. Like a good friend of mine says, "The rest of your life is the best of your life."

CHAPTER THIRTEEN

DON'T BE BOUND TO YOUR PAST...

*"One reason God created **time** was so there would be a place to bury the failures of the **past**." Author unknown*

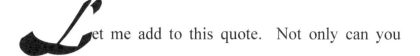et me add to this quote. Not only can you bury your past failures, you can also bury your past pains and hurts.

You cannot connect to your future until you disconnect from your past. I can't just live for my future. I must also enjoy my present life, my *here and now,* which helps me to prepare for my future at the same time. Life is made up of moments. Each moment creates a joy or a pain. Make no mistake about it; you live life moment by moment. You cannot live in your future. As soon as you enter your future it becomes your present. Each moment that you live in your present becomes your past. So no matter how you turn, you can only live in the present moment. You cannot start living when the bills are paid or the pain goes away. Learn to enjoy your present moment before it becomes your past. Your past is not some time or substance you can reclaim, but it is a valuable teacher. Learn from your past, live in the present, and use it wisely to prepare for your future.

You can't reenter your past or leap to your future. You live in your present called **today**! There is so much you can use from your past. As soon as you stop being hurt by the memories of your past, you can use the information that has been encoded in it to better equip yourself for your present and future.

"Brethren, I count not myself to have apprehended: but

this one thing I do, forgetting those things which are behind, and reaching forth unto those things which are before, I press toward the mark for the prize of the high calling of God in Christ Jesus." Philippians 3:13-14 KJV

STOP MAKING EXCUSES FOR YOUR LIFE AND CHANGE IT!

"What you're doing daily is deciding what you're becoming permanently." Mike Murdock

UNTIL YOU DESPISE YOUR PRESENT YOUR FUTURE WILL NEVER MATERIALIZE!

Change will never take place without transition. Change is circumstantial, but transition is psychological. If we try to make changes without transition, we'll at best rearrange things. No one will ever change as long as they defend their reasons as to why they can't change. Stop right now! No matter how bad your past was, or how bad things are right now, you can change if you want to. Transition is the key to change.

Circumstances can cause the desire to change, but unless we transition to a different mindset we will never really change. Transition is a passing from one condition, form, stage, activity or place to another; it is a shifting! If we want to really change, we must shift from one form or stage to something different. There must be an ending of one thing for the beginning of another to transpire. **END TO BEGIN**.

I believe there are three stages of change. The **first stage** must be *an ending*. The **second stage** is the hardest stage; it's the *letting go stage*. This is the stage where the old must be released even though the new hasn't fully arrived. It's the wilderness experience before you get to enjoy the fruits and blessings of the Promise Land. It's in this stage that most fail to make a complete transition. They begin to experience the loss of what was and have a hard time staying focused on what is coming. It's in this wilderness that the slavery of bondage must be dealt with. Past things must die and fall off so that they will not contaminate that which is made new.

"And no one pours new wine into old wineskins. If he does, the new wine will burst the skins, the wine will run out and the wineskins will be ruined. No, new wine must be poured into new wineskins. And no one after drinking old wine wants the new, for he says, 'The old is better.'" Luke 5:37-39 NIV

Old and new do not mix. As long as we try to hold onto the old, the new cannot come. In this middle stage we wrestle with old identities, old ideologies, old ideas, and old emotions. Some call this stage the "reconditioned stage" where we re-pattern ourselves for complete healing. Remember, it's the winter season that causes the trees to appear dead; but when spring arrives, the roots begin to heal and prepare themselves for their new season. It's during the night, while we sleep, that we are being disengaged from our failures and hurts, and engaged to prepare for the coming day's conquest.

The **third stage** is the final stage of transition, where we have *fully walked away* from our past, allowing sufficient time to heal and restore our inner man. Our minds have been cleansed and released from wrong thinking, and we are ready and prepared to venture into the newness of our lives.

Stop making excuses about your life and begin your transition today.

YOUR PAIN MAY NEVER LEAVE BUT CAN BE RELIEVED.

You will never completely separate from your past because without your past your life has no meaning. I believe that pain is not an enemy but an indicator. Pain lets you know that something isn't right and needs your attention.

A headache lets your body know that certain conditions, such as stress, have caused blood vessels in your head to constrict and cause you pain. The pain might be informing you that you can't take any more stress. If this pain and its causes are ignored, they will worsen. Taking medicine or relaxing in a darkened room for a while may ease or relieve your pain.

The memories of your past may always be around. Your past may have been very painful. The pain of those memories may never leave completely, but they can be relieved. When you allow yourself enough time to examine your wounds and learn from them, you will eventually move toward relieving your mind and heart of its hurt.

Remembering should be fruitful and not hurtful. Remembering certain things can cause you to be a better father… a better mother… a better friend. Your memories can teach you what *not* to do, which is as valuable as learning *what* to do. Take the time to decipher which steps or actions you need to take to relieve your pain. I promise that you will begin to experience a life that is not tormented by what has happened in your past.

"It Is Better To Take The Time To Consider, Than To Take The Time To Repent…" Matthew Henry

CHAPTER FOURTEEN

NEVER REWRITE YOUR THEOLOGY TO ACCOMMODATE A TRAGEDY

.

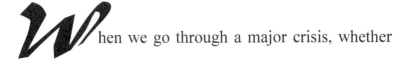hen we go through a major crisis, whether in our past or present, the tendency is to rewrite our theology to accommodate our tragedy. Say for instance, a person who stands on the Word of God for the healing of a loved one's terminal cancer confesses and believes God's will for healing, but the loved one dies. That person may change his theology from believing that healing *is* God's will, to adopting the phrase, *"If healing be God's will,"* because of what has happened. Healing *is* the will of God and so is death. It is appointed unto man to die, so death in Christ is also healing.

People who have had a past of pain and rejection get stuck on the *"If"* in the statement, *"If it be God's will."* When they receive positive statements such as, *"God loves you... it is the will of God that your life be full of joy... God desires to heal all, including you... God does want to bless you,"* they comfort themselves by adding the *"If"* just in case they should become disappointed again. They tend to rewrite theology to accommodate their insecurities because they have yet to experience the reality of God's will.

Can we comprehend all of God's truth? No. Sometimes we are just not going to understand. Perhaps I'm safe to assume that we don't understand God's ways most of the time. I don't want a God I can understand. I need God to be supernatural. I need Him to be bigger than what I can understand. **He is GOD!** Proverbs chapter three, verses five and six, tell us that *we are not to lean* *on our own understanding, but that we are to acknowledge God in all of our ways* (paraphrased).

I was suffering one of the worst pains of my life when this verse became a revealing light to me. I was trying to nurture my broken heart. Let me tell you, there's no man-made remedy for a truly broken and wounded heart. My life unraveled in a matter of days as I was attempting to make decisions that could cost me the rest of my life. I was going through a painful divorce while attending Bible College. It was during this stressful time that I had lost the god of my denomination and the god of my understanding. It was at this tender moment that I found the true God. The God of the Bible became *real* in the midst of my worst nightmare.

Through it all, God was God. Remember the song Andrae Crouch used to sing? *"Through it all... I've learned to depend upon His Words."* That's what happened. I survived the greatest season of my life by hanging onto what I already knew. God was bigger than my problem. I didn't rewrite my theology to accommodate my tragedy. I still believe that divorce is wrong. I still preach it isn't sanctioned by God, but I do preach that there is life after divorce. There is life after your pain. You just have to be willing to believe it and wait for it.

Stop telling your God how big your problems are, and start telling your problems how big your God is!

Don't rewrite your theology because of something that went wrong. Let me encourage you to avoid such practice. God has a plan and that plan is for you to be totally healed of your wounds. God's plan is for you to be prosperous and healed so that you can live a life full of joy as He has promised. No matter how much you've been hurt, expect a better life today… **Right now!**

You deserve the best of God as you begin to walk in His will and Word. Start living the life you were created to live, and stop living the life someone else has conditioned you to live.

Many of us have to face the fact that our problems have nothing to do with the enemy or God. They are the results of bad decisions. I've often heard Dr. Mike Murdock say, *"Decisions decide your wealth."* Replace the word wealth with any other word. It is your decisions that decide your future.

WRONG DECISIONS TRIGGER THE LAW OF UNINTENDED CONSEQUENCES.

Sometimes bad things result from wrong decisions. God never intended us to be destitute, but we must understand that wealth is the result of something. Life is a flow of cause and effect. Money is the effect of a cause. Health is the effect of eating right and exercising.

"For the law having a shadow of good things to come…" Hebrews 10:1 KJV

"But Christ being come an high priest of good things to come…" Hebrews 9:11 KJV

"How beautiful are the feet of them that preach the gospel of peace, and bring glad tidings of good

things!" Romans 10:15 KJV

God is in the good things of your life. As a matter of fact, take one vowel out of GOOD and you have GOD! *"Every good and perfect gift is from above and cometh down from the Father of lights......"* James 1:17 KJV

Understanding *the law of unintended consequences* is vital in avoiding pain. Each wrong decision triggers an unintended consequence or pain. For instance, a teenager goes to a party. He's been going to church his entire life, knows much of the Bible and prays daily. Yet he gets into a car knowing that the driver has had too much to drink. The driver exceeds the intended safe speed, looses control of the car which wraps around a tree, killing all. Could this have been God's intended plan for the boy or his friends? NO WAY! This was the result of a wrong decision.

Disobeying our laws can be costly. Disobeying God's laws are always costly!

Wrong decisions trigger *the law of unintended consequences*. Let me add yet another law; **"EVERY DECISION PRODUCES CONSEQUENCES,"** good or bad! Wrong decisions produce unintended problems. Stop blaming the devil and evaluate your decisions; they could be causing your problems.

What God has preordained can be postponed by your decisions. The good news is that God doesn't treat us as our sins deserve. Although wrong decisions produce unintended pain, unintended loss, and unintended crises, God still intends to bring into completion that which He has started. He is a GOOD GOD!

Allow me to quote a scripture that I love:

"The LORD is good to those who wait for Him, to the soul who seeks Him." Lamentations 3:25 NKJV

DECISIONS THAT CREATE CHANGE:

The access you decide to keep…
The addiction you decide to control…
The atmosphere you decide to create…
The attitude you decide to nurture…
The belief system you decide to cultivate…
The countenance you decide to reveal…
The commitment you decide to keep…
The courage you decide to show…
The crisis you decide to overcome…
The determination you decide to build….
The disappointment you decide to overcome…
The discouragement you decide to walk away from…
The effort you decide to use toward your success…
The education you decide to complete…
The faith you decide to build…
The enemy you decide to conquer…
The fight you decide to avoid…
The future you decide to pursue…
The fear you decide to face…
The offense you decide to forgive…
The wound you decide to let heal…
The pain you decide to fix…
The relationship you decide to keep…
The instruction you decide to follow…
The information you decide to pursue…

The mentor you decide to obey…
The seed you decide to sow…
The love you decide to give…
The friend you decide to forgive…
The financial mentor you decide to listen to…
The parent you decide to be…
The son or daughter you decide to be…
The sin you decide to walk away from…
The employee you decide to be…
The task you decide to take on…

Decisions are one of the most important ingredients to a happier and fuller life. There are many more decisions I could list, but do what I did. Build your own decision list.

CHAPTER FIFTEEN

WHERE DO YOU GO FROM HERE?

IT'S NOT JUST YOUR TIME,
IT'S YOUR TURN!

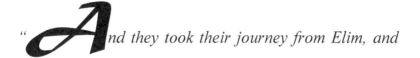 *"And they took their journey from Elim, and*

all the congregation of the children of Israel came unto the wilderness of Sin, which is between Elim and Sinai." Exodus 16:1 KJV

The Bible calls the place where the children of Israel were camping the "Wilderness of Sin." This place was located between Elim and Sinai.

"Elim" means *twisted* and "Sinai" means *uncertain.* If you're in the middle of a twisted and uncertain place where your thoughts have become so consumed with your situation and you wish you could return to the land of bondage and slavery, you are in the Wilderness of Sin. The real power of change begins in this valley of uncertainty. It's up to you to decide where you are going to go from here.

THREE ALTERNATIVES FOR THOSE IN THE WILDERNESS:

1. *You can go back to the land of bondage.*

2. *You can stay in the land of drought and comfort.*

3. *You can make haste to the warfare of increase and blessing.*

The only difference between a person who is wounded and a person who is healed is that one has decided to move beyond the wounds and into the promises of God.

There are no certainties in life, only opportunities. Open the door of possibility and start trekking to your promise land. Don't stay in your wilderness any longer. I know you're facing warfare to conquer your new place, but don't let it discourage you. Jesus has already won the victory for you. Your blessing is just around the corner of your decision to move into your promise land.

Your first alternative is to return to the predictability of slavery and bondage.

YOU MUST BE WILLING TO LEAVE THE LAND OF COMFORT, IF YOU DESIRE TO ENTER THE LAND OF PLENTY!

Many churchgoers today come to the saving knowledge of the cross, but few seem to cross through. We boast of our numbers of salvation, but what has become of all those saints after just a few months? They've returned to their Egypt. What seems to be driving these so called confessed people of faith back to the pit? I believe they've failed to change because they were neither challenged nor taught how to commit to change. They sense the presence of God, cry real tears, but refuse to face what has cost them so much deficiency and pain.

Emotional healing has become the greatest need of the modern-day church, but to be emotionally healed you must first be willing to look in the mirror of your life and reflect on what has caused you so much pain. This must be followed by an action or **biblical reaction** to what has hurt or wounded you. Perhaps it was a parent who rejected, betrayed or abused you; some anger or bitterness which drove you to hate life; a friend who lied about you, causing you to stop trusting people. There must be a godly response to the pains and wounds of your past so that you will not go back to the land of slavery.

Perhaps you suffered sexual abuse by someone you trusted or was raped by a stranger. Maybe you were religiously wounded or abused causing you to view church with a judgmental attitude and criticism. Whatever the cause of your hurt, **it must be countered by a godly reaction** and a willingness to let go of your past. If you don't release your past, you'll remain tied to it and eventually return to your old slavery and bondage.

Don't choose this tragedy. Yes, it may feel somewhat comfortable because it's familiar, but I promise you will never really leave your past. Forgive those who have betrayed you! Let go of the wounds of rejection, pain and false accusations. Walk free from the slave driver of insecurities and inferiorities.

Your second alternative is to stay in the wilderness of mediocrity and never move beyond your present.

There is an underlying attitude that seems to plague the church today. It is the posture of keeping one foot in the world while having the other in the church.

This is the comfort zone of complacency.

Complacency is to have an attitude of smugness and self-righteousness. These are the attitudes of those who have decided to stop growing. Many have attended church for so long that they've become accustomed to living on yesterday's manna and revelations. The church is full of people who haven't tasted a fresh word in so long that they resent anyone who has. They are those who survey leadership with a judgmental eye and resentful attitudes such as, *"who do you think you are?"*

Don't try to disciple the complacent. They won't hesitate to raze you with their words and lies. They are stuck in the land of drought and don't even know it. **Think about it!** Why is it that the church as a whole is the last to experience a **cutting edge** of **change and excellence**? I'll tell you why. Content desert dwellers have become so comfortable that they resist any change and seem content in the wilderness of yesterday, smug enough to die short of their promise land!

THE GREATEST ENEMY TO A PRESENT MOVE OF GOD IS THE LAST MOVE OF GOD...

If you are a desert dweller, leave the mirages and move on. **Make haste for change**. Get a fresh encounter with God. There is fresh bread in Bethlehem today! It is merely awaiting your arrival.

Your third alternative is to move with haste to the Promise Land!

This land flows with milk and honey. It flows with prosperity and increase. You've been designed by God to live on the **grapes of abundance, not the bowl of lack and mediocrity.**

Your promise land is centered in Jesus. Jesus is our Promise Land! Jesus is our spiritual rock. He is the water of change and joy from which our healing flows. He is our hope for a better tomorrow. He is the balm of Gilead. He is the Lion of the tribe of Judah. He is the Sword of the Spirit and the manifestation of God's love for us.

"For in Him we live and move and have our being, as also some of your own poets have said, 'For we are also His offspring.' Therefore, since we are the offspring of God, we ought not to think that the Divine Nature is like gold or silver or stone, something shaped by art and man's devising. Truly, these times of ignorance God overlooked, but now commands all men everywhere to repent, because He has appointed a day on which He will judge the world in righteousness by the Man whom He has ordained. He has given assurance of this to all by raising Him from the dead." Acts 17:28-31 NKJV

YOU'VE BEEN PREORDAINED FOR THE PROMISE LAND... YOUR PAST HAS NO DECISION ON WHERE YOU ARE GOING. YOU DO!

Stop sitting in your sin-dulled wilderness. Don't let man's doctrine cause you to accept a life of mediocrity. Get up and move with the redeemed! Get up right now and declare that you have been destined to eat the **grapes of blessing. IT'S TIME TO ENTER THE PROMISE LAND!**

KEYS THAT WILL SWING OPEN THE DOOR TO YOUR BLESSING:

Key One: CHRIST IS YOUR SPIRITUAL ROCK!

The people of the Old Testament drank from the rock but died in the wilderness. Drinking from the rock is not enough; you can still die in the wilderness. Merely drinking won't guarantee you the Promise Land, but your actions will!

"Moreover, brethren, I would not that ye should be ignorant, how that all our fathers were under the cloud, and all passed through the sea; And were all baptized unto Moses in the cloud and in the sea; And did all eat the same spiritual meat; And did all drink the same spiritual drink: for they drank of that spiritual Rock that followed them: and that Rock was Christ. But with many of them God was not well pleased: for they were overthrown in the wilderness. Now these things were our examples, to the intent we should not lust after evil things, as they also lusted. Neither be ye idolaters, as were some of them; as it is written, The people sat down to eat and drink, and rose up to play. Neither let us commit fornication, as some of them committed, and fell in one day three and twenty thousand. Neither let us tempt Christ, as some of them also tempted, and were destroyed of serpents. Neither murmur ye, as some of them also murmured, and were destroyed of the destroyer. Now all these things happened unto them for ensamples: and they are written for our admonition, upon whom the ends of the world are come. Wherefore let him that thinketh he standeth take heed lest he fall."
I Corinthians 10:1-12 KJV

Key Two: JESUS IS THE DOOR BY WHICH WE ENTER INTO THE PROMISE LAND.

There is no other door. Neither knowledge, nor works, nor anything else we do in church can take the place of the true door. That door is and must be Jesus.

"The Lord lives, Praise be to my Rock! Exalted be God, the Rock, of my salvation!" II Samuel 22:47 KJV

Key Three: JESUS IS THE ROCK OF REDEMPTION.

"Salvation is found in no one else, for there is no other name under heaven given to men by which we must be saved." Acts 4:12 KJV

We are changed and become new when we move and live in Jesus. This is not a onetime act. Churches have stopped teaching the progressive walk of change. We have to open the door of Jesus; to move and live in Him daily. Christ assigns the Holy Spirit to cleanse us when we make a total commitment. This cleansing must take place every day. You do not have to become saved every day, but you must bath and dress in Him daily. You must put on the whole Armor of God (Ephesians 6:14).

Key Four: JESUS IS THE ROCK OF RESTORATION.

"And a man shall be...as the shadow of a great rock in a weary land." Isaiah 32:2 KJV

Jesus is our protection! When the storms of life rage, He will be the Rock of shelter under which we can hide. He is our Rock of rest and peace (Psalm 37).

Key Five: JESUS IS THE ROCK OF RESOLUTION (STAMINA).

"He set my feet upon a rock, and established my goings." Psalm 40:2 KJV

Let's face it; the modern-day church has very little stamina. The minute the going gets tough, the Christian quits. They sign up for anything and show up for nothing! If they acted this way anywhere else they would be cut off or fired. However, in our modern-day, seeker-friendly church we just let people act and do as they want. Why? We are afraid that we might offend or lose them. Maybe *that's* the problem. Perhaps we should let them go!

We must give God first place in everything if we are to walk in a lasting relationship with Jesus. Christ must hold first place in our giving…in our living… in our singing… in our actions… and in our lifestyle. Any other place is a slap in God's face! When we put God first, He puts us first. The old saying applies, "He is either Lord of all, or not at all!"

Key Six: JESUS IS THE ROCK OF JOY.

"Let the inhabitants of the rock sing, let them shout from the top of the mountains." Isaiah 42:11 KJV

Some of us ruin our testimonies by wearing long unhappy faces. **Get excited about your life**. **Get excited about Jesus!**

REASONS TO BE EXCITED

The wealth of the wicked has been stored up for this day (Proverbs 13:22). The enemy is so mad, resisting your change, because he knows that God will prepare your increase by withdrawing your wealth from the devil's storehouse. This information alone should motivate you to become the best Christian... the best worshipper... the best giver you can possibly be.

Imagine how much seed you've planted in the unfertile ground of your bad decisions. Not only that, but how many seeds have you sown that have yet to come to fruition? What if God were to rekindle all of your dormant seeds? I am believing God with you right now that those dormant seeds are coming to fruition; that the seeds that you are presently sowing will be added to the seeds you have already sown to bring you an incredible harvest. If you don't like your harvest, change your seed. A seed that leaves your hand doesn't leave your life; it enters your future where it multiplies and brings you a harvest.

Confess this each day, **"Wealth of the Wicked Come to Me Now!**

CHAPTER SIXTEEN

GET YOUR EYES OFF YOUR PROBLEM AND ON YOUR PRAISE!

"When the Lord saw that Leah was unloved, He opened her womb…" Genesis 29:31 NKJV

*T*his moves me. God opened Leah's womb when

He saw that she was unloved.   Her womb became an expression of her pain. Many of us turn our womb into our wound when we have been hurt, rejected or have an imprinting of being unloved. The right thing to do is to open up your womb and give birth to your promise!

Rejection can last a long time in the mind. Jacob, of all people, should have been more sensitive to Leah. After all, he had first hand experience with being labeled and misunderstood. He had lived up to a bad name all of his life. His very name cried of his pain. The name 'Jacob' means trickster, con-artist, heel or hoof.   Everytime Jacob heard his name he was labeled a liar; the one who deceives.

Jacob had an older twin brother, Esau, who was shined upon by all; even his father. Isaac favored Esau and shunned Jacob. Imagine the pain of always feeling second and never measuring up.

Jacob worked seven years to marry Rachel, the daughter of Laban, who was beautiful in appearance. Her sister, Leah, didn't compare in beauty. Laban believed there would never be a man who would want to marry Leah so he decided to deceive Jacob. After Jacob worked seven years to marry Rachel, Laban sent Leah as the bride instead. Jacob consumated the marriage with the person he thought was Rachel on the wedding night. Here's where the story takes a twist…

Jacob had actually consummated his marriage with Leah, not Rachel! WOW... talk about being shallow. Here's a guy who was intimate with his wife without ever looking her in the face. He was so wounded he couldn't connect intimately with another. He laid with Leah and loved someone else.

Leah must have believed that Jacob would recognize her. How could anyone sleep with a person and not know who they are? The truth is Jacob did. He slept beside her all night and never entered into conversation with her. Not one time did Jacob try to connect with her and find out who she was and what she liked. That's what wounded people do. They make relationships without connections or commitment so they will not get hurt.

Can you imagine how Leah felt the next day when she heard Jacob screaming at her father, *"You deceived me! You tricked me! You gave me Leah, but I don't want her. I don't love her! I love Rachel!"* Once again Leah was compared to her sister. The husband she was in love with didn't want her. He wanted Rachel.

THE WOUNDED NEVER CONNECT OR COMMIT SO THAT THEY DON'T GET HURT AGAIN.

Since Jacob grew up hearing, *"Why can't you be more like your brother, Esau?"* he should have been able to understand Leah's pain.

I am sure her heart was broken and her mind was weakened. She must have felt like hiding in a cave and never coming out. Everyday many people like Leah are sitting in our churches, living in our neighborhoods and walking down our streets in their own cave of emotional wounds and imprintings. Their minds are imprisoned to their own thoughts and feelings.

God opened Leah's womb when He saw that she was unloved by her husband. People in biblical times would often name their children by what they were feeling or what was going on around them. Jacob was given his name because he was born hanging onto the heel of his brother, Esau.

Jacob didn't love Leah but continued to sleep with her. Leah was so engrossed in her rejection and pain that she reached out to Jacob through the names of her children. Her first child was named Reuben.

The name Reuben means, **SEE ME**! Leah was crying out, *"Jacob, why don't you ever look at me? Why don't you see me? Can't you see how much I love you? I need you to notice me!"*

There are two basic needs in humans:

1. *to be noticed*

2. *to have distinction*

Leah wanted to be noticed. She was living in a relationship where her love was not returned. She felt invisible; never being noticed by the object of her affection.

Jacob continued to lay with Leah without showing her love. Leah gave birth to her second son, whom she named Simeon.

The name Simeon means, **HEAR ME!** She was crying out again, *"Why don't you hear me? When I talk you stare off as if I'm not even in the room."* Many women cry the tears of not being heard. I can imagine the tears streaming down Leah's face. Her heart was broken and no one could fix it.

Leah continued expressing her pain but to no avail. Jacob never changed.

While Leah laid in her chambers she heard Jacob's foot steps coming down the hallway towards her. Her heart raced in her chest and her mind went crazy. She loved Jacob, but all she could do was birth his children. Her open womb was his only attraction to her. Jacob would lay with her and leave. Talk about feeling used and abused. She gave Jacob what he wanted, but he never considered her needs and wants. She conceived Jacob's third son. She named him Levi.

Levi means, **JOIN ME!** She was asking for agreement and for connection from Jacob. She needed to know that she was important enough for Jacob to connect with her. *"Jacob, do you know my interests, do you know what I like? Do you even know what I want in life?"* Isn't that what we all really want, someone to know us? Someone to connect with us deeper than just in shallow moments of stimulation.

> **STOP TELLING GOD HOW BIG YOUR PROBLEMS ARE AND START TELLING YOUR PROBLEMS HOW BIG YOUR GOD IS!**

I want to interject a point before I move forward. I wonder if God was trying to give us an example of how we treat Him? Do we actually see Him, hear Him or even really connect to Him?

The only thing on Leah's mind as she gave birth to her sons was her pain and rejection. She was so consumed with trying to get Jacob to see her, hear her and join her that she lost her identity. King David experienced the same issue. He was so wounded that he loved those who hated him and hated those who loved him.

Life continued for Leah. Jacob's mode of operation didn't change. He would lay with her then leave her to finish the night alone. Something changed in Leah's mind when she conceived her fourth child. Four is the number of transition. Through the nightmare of her reality, Leah transitioned in her mind. She made the decision to take her mind off of her problems, to stop trying to please a man and to start thinking about the God over her situation.

Stop telling God how big your problem is and start telling your problem how big your God is.

Leah moved into a different mind set. She decided to stop living in the wound and turn her wound into the womb to birth her future.

She delivered her fourth son, held him high and screamed **JUDAH!**

The name Judah means, **GOD BE PRAISED!** That was the proof that Leah had changed. She decided to stop looking at Jacob for what she needed and started looking at God. Her focus shifted and her passion changed. Her dreams were coming back. She decided to no longer live in the prison of what another person thought. She was going to live a life that praised God. She turned her eyes off of herself and onto her PRAISE!

I believe you are making a shift right now. If you are tired of living your life for someone else, then do what Leah did! Turn your life into a praising life. I'm talking about having a *"Crazy Praise."* The enemy can't stop you. He can never lock you up in the prison of loneliness again. Send up Judah! Send up your praise. Get your eyes off of you and put your eyes on your praise. Open your mouth and shout, JUDAH! Go ahead, do it right now. Shout JUDAH! Let the enemy know that you are a praiser.

Leah was visited by Jacob once again and conceived her fifth son. Five is the number of favor. Leah entered a season of favor.

She named her fifth son Isaacar, which means **REWARD.**

She conceived her sixth son and named him Zebulun. The name Zebulun means **HONOR.** Leah finished her life with reward and honor. How did this happen? She decided to get her eyes off of her wound and back onto her womb.

Your past may have "cut" you, but it isn't your wound. It is your womb! Your praise is connected to your reward and honor.

On Jacob's death bed he said to his sons, *"Don't bury me in Egypt. Bury me in the land of Canaan; in the cave where I have buried Leah. Isaac, my father, is also buried there beside his love, Rebecca. Bury me beside Leah for all eternity because I loved her."* (Genesis 49:13 *paraphrased*)

Wow, I love this story! Leah finally got what she desired. She has been laying beside her husband for thousands of years. Jacob finally realized how much Leah meant to him.

CHAPTER SEVENTEEN

LEARN HOW TO REST WHILE BEARING YOUR BURDEN

GOD'S REST STOP ON THE ROAD TO GREATNESS

"*Then the LORD said to Joshua, "Today I have rolled away the reproach of Egypt from you." So the place has been called Gilgal to this day."* *Joshua 5:9 NIV*

Many fail to walk in their assignment because they are still walking in the guilt and shame of their past. The word reproach in the Hebrew means disgrace, shame, exposure and guilt. The enemy will use our mistakes to keep us anchored to the feelings of guilt and shame.

> **MAN IS THE ONLY CREATURE THAT CRIES OVER ITS MISTAKES**

"There is therefore now no condemnation to those who are in Christ Jesus, who do not walk according to the flesh, but according to the Spirit." *Romans 8:1 NKJV*

Man is the only creature on the planet that I know of that blushes when they are embarrassed or exposed. Man is the only creature that cries over mistakes. If we had to live like the animal kingdom, we would die of starvation. When an animal can't overpower another animal, it doesn't sit around and cry about it. It doesn't call up all the other animals to share why it's hungry. Animals find what they can conquer so they will survive!

The most overlooked emotional wounds in counseling are the feelings of shame and guilt. If distress is the effect of suffering, then shame and guilt are the effects of indignity, transgression and alienation. Many are suffering from past failures and mistakes, and they lack the ability to face them. Many are ashamed of being ashamed. When they come to us we want to talk about drugs, mistakes and even attempt to cast spirits off them. The truth they need to know is that they are okay, and that God isn't holding them accountable for what was.

People who are suffering from the spirit of shame often equate that feeling with being unlovable, worthless, unredeemable or cut off!

Shame is often experienced in the mind as a voice that screams louder than good and acceptable thoughts. That inner voice is a critical voice that judges whatever we do wrong. It speaks of inferiority and worthlessness.

This inner voice can repeat words spoken in the past by people such as parents, teachers, relatives or peers. This voice says things such as, **"You are horrible, selfish, ugly, fat and stupid."** These voices can speak so loud that you are unable to hear the loving voice of the Holy Spirit who is trying to bring peace among chaos.

"It takes courage to call order to chaos..."

What are you hearing? **"You idiot! Why did you do that? Can't you do anything right? You should be ashamed of yourself."**

These words are internalized in your mind. They are expressed outwardly through the feelings of anger, fear, sadness or vulnerability. They may be met with shaming reproaches such as, **"Pull yourself together," "Don't be a cry baby," "Stop crying or I'll give you something to cry about," "Stop being afraid," "You make me sick," "I wish I had never had you," "Why can't you be like..."** We must understand that pride is also a feeling that is often met with shameful condemnation such as, **"Who do you think you are? Do you think you're too big to be corrected?"**

Remember, these feelings are birthed from the voices of your past. This shaming inner voice can do more damage to your self esteem than if someone beat you with a stick. Bruises and cuts heal faster than the internal wounds caused by words and shame. What we tend to do is live in a self critical world. We tell ourselves we are stupid, unreachable, show offs, selfish and no good. As a result, we are walking in a sea of negative thoughts about ourselves and those connected to us. We evaluate everything with a negative mindset and wonder why no one wants to be around us.

This inner critical voice makes it almost impossible for one to do anything right. It will tell you that you are **too aggressive or that you're not aggressive enough; that you're too selfish or that you let people walk all over you.** What voices are you listening to?

Shame is defined as *a painful feeling of having lost the respect of others because of the improper behavior or incompetence of oneself or another; a feeling of dishonor or disgrace.*

Shame entered mankind for the first time when Adam sinned in the Garden of Eden. I don't believe that Adam was ashamed of being naked as much as he was ashamed for being guilty of doing wrong. When God showed up, Adam immediately hid. This was the first reaction   to   shame   and   guilt.

God asked Adam, *"Where are you? Why are you hiding from me? Have you done what I've asked you not to do?"* Disobedience always produces shame. Adam answered God, *"Yes, we are naked,"* or better, we are ashamed. Let me tell you what entered mankind that day. Adam was really saying, *"We are **alienated, inadequate, helpless, powerless, defenseless, weak, insecure, uncertain, shy, ineffectual, inferior, flawed, exposed, unworthy, hurt, intimidated, defeated, rejected, dumb, rebuffed, stupid, bizarre, odd, peculiar, and different.** God, we are nothing like You at all!"*

SHAME TARGETS THE DEEPEST PLACES IN MAN! Shame is an inner torment, a sickness of the soul. This is why we need Jesus. This is why we must receive the Son of God as our doorway out of our shame, our guilt and our pain

DON'T MOVE, DON'T TEACH, AND DON'T DO ANYTHING UNTIL YOU ARE HEALED.

The worst thing you can do in the church is promote someone who is still wounded and who is still fighting the symptoms of shame and guilt.

"And after the whole nation had been circumcised, they remained where they were in camp until they were healed." Joshua 5:8 NIV

After the wilderness, God told Joshua to re-circumcise all the men. He then instructed them to stay put so He could roll away their shame and guilt. Why? Because when you haven't dealt with your past the enemy will most assuredly use it against you.

HOW TO HAVE A JERICHO HOUR:

1. Have an encounter with God that is bigger than your past.
2. Have an exchange that will open the door of your harvest.   3. Begin to sow seeds right now for your future.
4. Have an invasion that will tear down the walls of bondage
    and fear.

GOD TEARS DOWN WALLS, BUT MEN TAKE CITIES!

God tears down the walls, but it's up to us to take back what the enemy has stolen.

It's time for you to walk healed of your wounds. The mess you had to live through is your message to help others survive.

You are the best of God. You are about to experience the healing waters of the river of life. Everywhere the river flows the fish live. Get ready to live! Start living and let determination overcome your damages.

YOU ARE SAVED BUT DAMAGED NO MORE!

CONCLUSION

It is my prayer and desire that each of my books will help people grow on a daily basis.

Call my ministry for reduced prices if you wish to share this book with anyone who is suffering from emotional wounds. I've labored to make it easy to read.

If you are ever in the Hickory or Charlotte area of North Carolina, I would be delighted and blessed if you would visit us at one of The **Favor Center Churches.** Visit my website at **www.thefavorcenter.net** for more information.

You matter dearly to me. I am honored to have been placed into your life to help you succeed in everything God has destined for you.

Sincerely,
Dr. Jerry Grillo

MAY I INVITE YOU TO MAKE JESUS CHRIST LORD OF YOUR LIFE?

The Bible says, "That if you will confess with your mouth the Lord Jesus, and will believe in your heart that God raised Him from the dead, you will be saved. For with the heart man believes unto righteousness; and with the mouth confession is made for salvation." Romans 10:9, 10

PRAY THIS PRAYER WITH ME TODAY:

"Dear Jesus, I believe that You died for me, and that You rose again on the third day. I confess to You that I am a sinner. I need Your love and forgiveness. Come into my life, forgive my sins, and give me eternal life. I confess You now as my Lord and Savior. Thank You for my salvation! I walk in Your peace and joy from this day forward. Amen!"

Signed_____Date _____

☐   Yes, I would like to be put on your mailing list.

Name_____

Address_____

City_____State_____Zip_____Phone:_____

Email:_____

FOGZONE MINISTRIES
P.O. Box 3707, Hickory N.C. 28603
1.888.328.6763 Fax: 828.325.4877
WWW.FOGZONE.NET

WHAT OTHERS ARE SAYING

Dr. Jerry Grillo lives what he teaches. It has been my privilege to be his personal friend for a number of years. He is a living example of a victorious leader. His church is a victorious church. If you can't succeed under this man of God you can't succeed anywhere. His revelation is life's fresh air in a stagnant world. He is one of the happiest and most exciting leaders I have known through my thirty-eight years of world evangelism. It is my privilege to recommend any book he has written.

Dr. Mike Murdock
The Wisdom Center
Dallas, TX

Dr. Jerry Grillo is truly a gift from God to my life. I love his passion, his purity and his painstaking commitment to purpose. It is very obvious that he loves the God he preaches to us about. Should you ever have the privilege of peaking into this life, you would know without a doubt he's one of God's favorites. Bishop Grillo, what a wonderful refreshing, what a wonderful friend!

Pastor Sheryl Brady
Sheryl Brady Ministries

Bishop Grillo is fast becoming a leading voice of authority... Having him minister at our Emotional Healing Conference became a valuable training session to our leadership and a needed breakthrough to many of our members. To say that Bishop Grillo is qualified to pen these pages would be an understatement. You hold in your hand a key to unlocking the life that God desires for you. I dare you to turn these pages with even the least little bit of expectation and watch as God begins to show out in your life!

Bishop Jeff Poole
New Hope International
Warner Robins, GA

TO INVITE DR. JERRY GRILLO TO SPEAK AT YOUR NEXT CHURCH CONFERENCE, BUSINESS MEETING OR TO SCHEDULE TELEVISION OR RADIO INTERVIEWS

WRITE TO:

FOGZONE MINISTRIES
P.O. BOX 3707
HICKORY, NC. 28603

OR EMAIL: FZM@FOGZONE.NET

FAX INVITATION TO 828-325-4877

OR CALL 1-888 FAVOR ME

END NOTES

Chapter 6: "Your Mind is your world." *Some of this chapter was taken from the The Nemours Foundation website.*

Chapter 11: "Bitterness" *some of the material came from one of Dr. Mike Murdock's mini books. Because people matter to him, He allowed me to use his material for this book.*

STAY**CONNECTED,**
BE**BLESSED.**

From thoughtful articles to powerful newsletters, videos and more, www.fogzone.net is full of inspirations that will give you encouragement and confidence in your daily life.

AVAILABLE ON WWW.FOGZONE.NET
to Join the FAVORNATION and receive a weekly update
text the word "FAVORNATION" to 22828

LAUNCH
PASTORS AND LEADERSHIPS

Weekly Conference Calls from Dr. Grillo will help you grow in your relationship with the Lord and equip you to be everything God intends you to be.

Wednesday @ 12:00pm EST

Call: (712) 432-0075   Playback: (712) 432-1085
access CODE 138750#   access CODE 138750#

 Dr. Jerry Grillo
STREAMING

Miss your local church service? Watch Dr. Grillo online, and see him LIVE

Sundays @ 10:30am EST & Wednesday @ 7:00pm EST

 Dr. Jerry Grillo
VIDEO ARCHIVE

The Video Archive is a great way to watch Dr. Grillo where you want and when you want. Go to www.drjerrygrillo.com and click on "Encore"

CONNECT WITH US

Join the FAVORNATION on your favorite social network

PUT DR. GRILLO IN YOUR POCKET

Get the inspiration and encouragement from Dr. Jerry Grillo on your iPhone, iPad or Android device! Our website will stream on each platform.

Thanks for helping us make a difference in the lives of millions around the world.

WWW.FOGZONE.NET

RELEASING THE **F.O.G.**
FAVOR OF GOD

Dr. Jerry A. Grillo, Jr.
Author, Pastor, and Motivational Speaker

Favor Conferences - Dr. Grillo is able to minister to many during seminars and conferences throughout America and around the world. Dr. Grillo's heart is to help encourage and strengthen Senior Pastors and leaders.

Books - Dr. Grillo has written over twenty -five books including best sellers, "Saved But Damaged," and, "Pray for Rain." Dr. Grillo sows his book, "Daddy God," into Prison Ministries across the country; this book shows the love of God as our Father.

Internet and Television - Dr. Grillo is anointed to impart the wisdom of God on Favor, Overflow and Emotional Healing. Online streaming and television has made it possible for Dr. Grillo to carry this message around the world into homes and lives that he would otherwise not be able to reach.

Dr. Jerry Grillo
STREAMING
Miss your local church service?
Watch Dr. Grillo online, and
see him LIVE
Sundays @ 10:30am EST &
Wednesday @ 7:00pm EST

@BISHOPGRILLO
/BISHOPGRILLO
GODSTRONGTV

Join the
FAVORNATION
by texting
FAVORNATION
to "22828"

MEDIA & DESIGNS
FOGZONE PUBLISHING
WWW.FOGZONEDESIGNS.COM

WWW.DRJERRYGRILLO.COM